TO ALL WHO

UNDERSTAND THESE TIMES

AND WISELY PREPARE

WHEN ALL PLANS FAIL

WORKBOOK

PAUL R. WILLIAMS, MD

WHEN ALL PLANS FAIL WORKBOOK by Paul R. Williams, M.D.
Published by Mountain View Publishing, LLC
Pisgah Forest, North Carolina, USA

Unless otherwise noted, all Scripture quotations are taken from *New International Version*®. Copyright © 1973, 1978, 1984, 2010, 2011 by International Bible Society. Used by permission. All rights reserved.

Scripture quotations marked NKJV are from the *New King James Version*. Copyright © 1979, 1980, 1982 by Thomas Nelson, Inc. Used by permission. All rights reserved.

Scripture quotations marked TLB are from *The Living Bible*. Copyright © 1971. Used by permission of Tyndale House Publishers, Inc., Wheaton, IL 60189. All rights reserved.

Design Director: Justin Evans
Cover design by Justin Evans

Visit the author's website: www.whenallplansfail.com

ISBN: 978-0-9965834-0-4

This publication contains the opinions and ideas of its author. It is intended to provide helpful and informative material on the topics covered in this book. It is sold with the understanding that the author and publisher are not rendering medical services. It is suggested that doctors and/or other appropriate healthcare professionals be consulted on all medical matters that require medical attention, diagnosis or treatment. The author and publisher are not rendering any professional legal or professional financial service or advice. The author and publisher specifically disclaim all responsibility for any liability, loss or risk, personal or otherwise, that is incurred as a consequence directly or indirectly, of the use and application of any of the contents of this book.

The author has made every effort to provide accurate telephone numbers and Internet addresses at the time of publication, neither the publisher nor the author assumes any responsibility for errors or for changes that occur after publication.

First Edition, revised and updated

15 16 17 18 19 - 987654321
Printed in the United States of America

CONTENTS

PART 4: EVACUATION READINESS

PART 5: FITNESS & NUTRITION

PART 6: HOME SECURITY

PART 7: APPENDICES

INTRODUCTION

This workbook is designed to supplement the book *When All Plans Fail*. As you fill out the information on these pages, you will be creating your own personal **Disaster Preparedness Plan** that will reflect the unique needs of you and your family.

Some of the information in this *When All Plans Fail Workbook* is taken directly from the book by the same name, though I have added supplementary information, lists and tables when deemed necessary. The workbook places all the check lists together in one place and streamlines the information for easy use and referencing.

You should have more than one copy of portions of your **Disaster Preparedness Plan** in a personal notebook. Make photocopies of the pages you desire to keep in different places. For example, you may want to keep one not only in your home, but also at work and in your car. You may even want to share one with a family member not living with you or a trusted friend.

PREPARING FOR DISASTERS IS NOT A ONE-TIME EVENT

Constantly be on the alert for new information and added to your preparedness plan. Remember, for greater peace of mind, prepare yourself and your family **NOW** for potential natural and man-made disasters.

GET YOUR NOTEBOOK READY

+ Buy a 3-ring loose leaf notebook.

+ Buy plastic sheets designed for 3-ring notebooks. Using these plastic sheets will protect your plan and it will not be necessary to use a 3-hole punch for your documents.

+ Buy dividers and/or tabs to indicate the different sections for easy referencing.

SUGGESTIONS ON HOW TO USE THE WORKBOOK

+ Just GET **STARTED!**

+ Do not feel as if you have to do all the suggestions

+ Go through the workbook to get an "overview" of all that is recommended and obtained different items as you can afford them.

+ Try **NOT** to do everything by yourself. Involve the whole family.

+ Don't feel compelled to follow any particular order in getting supplies. Just check things off when they're purchased or an action item is completed.

+ At least assemble the items in the Bare-Bones Personal Emergency Kit and have some means of making your drinking water safe in an emergency.

+ Make disaster preparedness into a game with smaller children.

+ Share what you learn with your family and friends.

SYMBOLS USED IN WORKBOOK

 CHECKLISTS AND TO DO ITEMS

 CRITICAL INFORMATION

 WHERE TO FIND INFORMATION IN
WHEN ALL PLANS FAIL

 WEBSITE LINKS FOR MORE INFORMATION

 IMPORTANT PHONE NUMBERS

THE SENSIBLE MAN

"A sensible man watches for problems ahead and prepares to meet them. The simpleton never looks, and suffers the consequences."

Proverbs 27:12 (TLB)

FOR WANT OF A NAIL

For want of a nail, the shoe was lost.
For want of a shoe, the horse was lost.
For want of a horse, the rider was lost.
For want of a rider, the battle was lost.
And all for the want of a horseshoe nail.

Benjamin Franklin

MAXIMS TO REMEMBER

"To fail to plan is to plan to fail."

"An ounce of prevention is worth a pound of cure."

Benjamin Franklin

HOPE

BASIC READINESS

OVERVIEW

IN PART ONE you will:

+ Make a Disaster Planning Schedule to involve the entire family.

+ Make an Emergency Contact list for use at home, work and to place in your Grab-and-Go bags.

+ Create a Family Health Information-Quick Reference list to have pertinent health information readily available when making emergency calls.

+ Learn about the Emergency Alert System, Wireless Emergency Alerts, NOAA Weather Radios and broadcast emergency phone messaging systems.

+ Learn about steps to take to make your home safer and avoid potential problems through such things as doing a Home Hazard Hunt.

+ Identify your "Horses" – disasters common to your area where you live.

ESTABLISH A SCHEDULE

Set time each week that you will set aside time for disaster planning. Do at least one-half hour, though 1-2 hours per week would be better. Include all family members at least once each month. Get each family member to "buy-in" to the schedule that is set. Be sure children are included in age appropriate ways. Make planning a game for the children. Do not instill fear! Go shopping as a family to acquaint each family member of the various choices and let the children participate and learn through the process.

As simple as it may seem, write down on this page what days and times you will commit to for disaster planning. Putting this in writing will help you keep your commitment and also be a reminder to your family of what has been planned.

Also, assign tasks to different family members so that the task does not fall on just one individual. For example, if a child is old enough, assign him or her to obtain copies of the school policies on emergencies such as fires, tornadoes as well as other important policies relating to care of your child(ren).

DISASTER PLANNING SCHEDULE

I commit to set aside time M T W TH F SAT SUN (circle) each week for disaster planning.

I have scheduled the whole family to get together on:

_____ (dates and times)

_____ (dates and times)

_____ (dates and times)

_____ (dates and times)

POST THE DATES AND TIMES FOR THE FAMILY TO
GET TOGETHER IN A CONSPICUOUS PLACE
AS A REMINDER!

EMERGENCY CONTACT NUMBERS
REMEMBER LOCAL AND NATIONAL ASSISTANCE CODES

Dial 211   Connects callers to health and human services in your local area. This is a non-emergency number, but is an excellent source to learn where you can find local assistance for special needs that you or a family member might have during an emergency. Seventy-eight percent of the US has 211 available.

Dial 411   Telephone directory assistance

Dial 511   America's traveler information: local traffic and road conditions given on these calls; Also can go online for more extensive information at:

 www.511.com.

Dial 911   Emergency calls connect to police, highway patrol, fire departments, hospitals, etc. Land line is best if available. It will identify your location.

POISON

If someone has been poisoned, or you suspect someone has been poisoned, immediately call:

National Capital Poison Center   1-800-222-1222

www.poison.org

National Battery Ingestion Hotline   1-202-625-3333
Call collect if necessary. Button batteries are a major hazard with many devices using them. There has been a national hotline set up to give advice should one be swallowed.

EMERGENCY CONTACT LIST

Police: _____

Highway Patrol: _____

Fire: _____

Doctor(s): _____

_____

Hospital: _____

Schools: _____

_____

Electric utility: _____

Gas company: _____

Water company: _____

EMERGENCY CONTACT LISTS GO:

- in your personal notebook
- beside your phones at home
- in your Grab-and-Go bags
  - home (family and personal)
  - car
  - workplace
- in your personal pouch

FAMILY HEALTH INFORMATION
QUICK REFERENCE

Though the following information may be duplicated in other places, I recommend that some health information for each family member be listed in this emergency contact section. This is particularly critical for children, elderly and handicapped family members.

Place this information with your EMERGENCY CONTACT LIST. This is a handy place to have basic family medical information if an emergency call needs to be made. This will be of great help should a babysitter or someone unfamiliar with the family needs to make an emergency call.

For each family member write-down:

- Name
- Age
- Height
- Weight
- Allergies
- Medications and the dosage of the medications

Doctors' offices, pharmacies, and emergency personnel will need to know this information.

You may want to purchase a memory C.A.R.E. wrist band for you and each family member.(Easily enter all family health information on the user-friendly software.) This can be particularly helpful for elderly and handicapped family members.

 Available at many drug stores and at:
www.medicalhistorybracelet.com

FAMILY HEALTH QUICK REFERENCE INFORMATION
FOR EMERGENCY CALLS

Health Insurance Company (name/phone number):_____

Group Number:_____

ID number: _____

_____

_____

_____

_____

_____

_____

_____

_____

_____

_____

_____

EMERGENCY EARLY WARNING SYSTEMS

EMERGENCY ALERT SYSTEM

The *Emergency Alert System* (EAS) can address the entire nation on very short notice in case of national emergencies. *Wireless Emergency Alerts* (WEA) are emergency messages sent by authorized government alerting authorities through your mobile carrier.

 www.fcc.gov

NOAA WEATHER RADIO

Known as the "Voice of NOAA's National Weather Service," *National Weather Radio* (NWR) is provided as a public service by the National Oceanic and Atmospheric Administration (NOAA). The NWR requires a special radio receiver or scanner capable of picking up the signal.

 www.weather.gov/nwr

INTEGRATED PUBLIC ALERT AND WARNING SYSTEM (IPAWS)

IPAWS provides public safety officials with an effective way to alert and warn the public about serious emergencies using the Emergency Alert System (EAS), Wireless Emergency Alerts (WEA), the National Oceanic and Atmospheric Administration (NOAA) Weather Radio and other public alerting systems from a single interface.

 www.fema.gov/integrated-public-alert-warning-system

BROADCAST PHONE MESSAGING

There are several commercial emergency notification services that can provide emergency notification using voice broadcasting and interactive voice response systems (IVR, which is a system that allows a person to make a selection from a voice menu). Literally thousands of people can be notified by phone in minutes and be warned of blizzards, forest fires, toxic spills, etc. These messages can be delivered to special TTY / TDD phones for the deaf and hearing impaired. Two such services are:

 www.911broadcast.com
www.databasesystemscorp.com

EMERGENCY WARNING SYSTEMS WHERE YOU LIVE

(Circle all that apply and writing others not listed below.)

EAS — Emergency Alert System

NOAA– NWR — National oceanic and atmospheric administration national weather radio

IPAWS — Integrated Public Alert Warning System

Broadcast Phone Messaging — if you do not have this service, share this information with your community leaders.

Sirens

Other: _____

_____

NOAA WEATHER RADIOS

NOAA broadcast cannot be heard on simple AM/FM receivers. That is why you need to have NOAA Weather Radio receivers for:

- your **home**
- your **car**
- your **workplace**
- and put one in the family **Grab-and-Go bag**.

Most radio models use batteries or have hand and/or solar rechargeable capabilities. The majority of major retail outlets carry these radios.

MITIGATION: BEFORE DISASTERS STRIKE

For every disaster there are four aspects of preparedness: mitigation, preparation, response and recovery. Mitigation is best. Many disasters can be avoided by taking steps to prevent potential problems. The list of possible steps to take to mitigate various disasters could be a book in itself. I am using these two pages to challenge you to think about ways to minimize your exposure to potential disasters and to provide internet resources for you to explore to mitigate various potential problems.

I have come across an important website of the **Institute for Business and Home Safety**. This resource provides both home and business owners step-by-step information to help you prepare for disasters most likely to occur in your area where you live. They have a ZIP CODE TOOL that allows you to get advice specific to your area. They also provide routine maintenance information to help minimize losses of both property and time.

 www.disastersafety.org

HOME HAZARD HUNT

In her book, *Organize for Disaster*, Judith Kolberg includes a great section on mitigation and home hazard hunt. Go through your home and declutter your home to mitigate against injury and destruction during a disaster.

The better you prepare, the better your response will be should an emergency arise. Your recovery phase will be shorter and you will have experienced less loss.

MAINTAIN YOUR STATE OF READINESS

You may initially plan well for all four steps for each type of hazard, but failed to maintain the state of readiness. Maintenance is key to excellent preparedness!

EXAMPLES OF MITIGATION STEPS TO TAKE

- Move old lumber away from the side of your home to mitigate against attracting termites as well as decrease any fire hazard.
- Move or secure lawn, deck or pool furniture if high winds are possible
- Regularly rotate food/water supplies to keep up-to-date to prevent spoilage.
- Rotate medications to prevent medications from becoming outdated, ineffective or worse, harmful.
- Avoid letting home, auto or life insurances lapse or you may experience significant loss.
- Secure boats or put in storage if storms are predicted.
- Know how to cut off utilities in an emergency to minimize damages or possible losses.
- Trim trees and shrubs that might damage home if a severe storm hits.
- Use non-inflammable materials to build your home or place of business.
- Place heavy or breakable items on lower shelves.
- Store poisonous or harmful household cleaning supplies in a "childproof" place or container.
- Replace any damaged electrical plugs, cords or sockets.

TIPS FOR HOME AND MANUFACTURED HOME SAFETY

MANUFACTURED HOME SAFETY CHECKLIST

 www.disastersafety.org/?s=manufactured+homes

SAFER HOME CHECKLIST

 www.disastersafety.org/?s=safer+home

KEEPING YOUR HOME SAFE WHEN YOU ARE AWAY

 www.disastersafety.org/?s=KEEPING+YOUR+HOME +SAFE+WHEN+YOU+ARE+AWAY

IDENTIFY DISASTERS COMMON TO WHERE YOU LIVE

Circle the hazard risk level of all the disasters on the facing page. Suggestion: don't just rely on your own knowledge, but ask local authorities as well, particularly if you have not lived very long in your current location.

Take into consideration other hazards about which you should be informed, even if you do not specifically run much risk where you live, since most people travel and may face hazards while away from home. I recommend you include in your notebook all the major hazards including fire, flooding, hurricanes, tornadoes, thunderstorms, coronal mass ejections (CMEs), extreme cold and extreme heat even if some may not be common to where you live.

Arrange the hazards in your notebook from highest risk levels to lowest risk levels. Use tabs with name of the hazards to quickly identify where the preparedness guidelines are located for each hazard.

FAMILY REVIEW OF HAZARDS

As a family, go over each of the hazards and review, discussing matters at age-appropriate levels. Make sure everyone understands his or her roles if specific assignments are given to different family members.

The information from Appendix A in *When All Plans Fail*: Hazard Specific Preparedness Guidelines has been expanded in this workbook. Each hazard is listed on a separate page in the workbook for ease in copying.

DISASTERS COMMON TO WHERE YOU LIVE

Circle Appropriate Hazard Level Where You Live

Natural Hazards		Risk Level	
Fires	H	M	L
Floods	H	M	L
Hurricanes	H	M	L
Tornadoes	H	M	L
Thunderstorms/lightning	H	M	L
Winter storms/ice storms	H	M	L
Extreme Cold	H	M	L
Extreme Heat	H	M	L
Earthquakes	H	M	L
Wildfires	H	M	L
Landslides and debris flow	H	M	L
Volcanoes	H	M	L
Tsunamis	H	M	L

Technological Hazards		Risk Level	
Hazardous materials incidents	H	M	L
Nuclear power plants	H	M	L

Once you have identified the types of hazards you are most likely to encounter, make a copy of these specific preparedness guidelines for each hazard identified. Insert this information in your notebook.

 See chapter 3, "Horses or Zebras," in *When All Plans Fail*.

WHO YA GONNA CALL?

"He will call upon me, and I will answer him;
I will be with him in trouble,
I will deliver him and honor him."

Psalm 91:15

EMERGENCY COMMUNICATION

OVERVIEW

IN PART TWO you will:

+ Make a contact card for each family member.

+ Decide where your family will meet if evacuation is necessary.

+ Have medical release forms filled out for each child and on file at school.

+ Obtain prepaid phone cards for family members for emergencies.

+ Have recent close up photos of each family member for emergencies.

+ Share your family communication information with all family members.

+ Consider forming a Family Emergency Communications Network.

+ Consider forming a Neighborhood Emergency Communications Network.

FAMILY COMMUNICATIONS PLAN AND CHECK LIST

Family communication in time of crisis is vital. The contact card on the facing page is primarily for family communication for disasters close to home that affect family members that live in proximity to each other. Either create your own emergency contact cards or go to:

 www.ready.gov/sites/default/files/documents/ files/Family_Emegency_Plan.pdf

ADDITIONAL COMPONENTS

Pre-arranged authorization for family or friends to pick up children at school should you not be able to if a disaster strikes;

Medical release forms for each child to be on file with the schools. These forms need to be notarized giving permission for emergency medical care to be given. Obtain free forms online or from your schools;

Prepaid phone cards for each family member for emergencies;

Pictures of family members should family members become separated;

Share this family communication information with family members not living in the same area. Put plan in place to notify family when safe.

Place **hard copies** of the family communication plan in water proof containers into your emergency kits!

MAJOR NATIONAL CATASTROPHE SCENARIO

Make family plans on where the family would try to meet in the event of a major national catastrophe and normal communication channels are disrupted. If you and your family have to evacuate, leave a note in your home where you plan to go.

FAMILY COMMUNICATIONS PLAN AND CHECK LIST

Fill out the **contact card** information below for each family member and keep with him or her at all times. Put this information on a card that will easily fit into a wallet, purse or pocket. Laminate the cards to make them more durable. These cards should be carried by each family member at all times. Place this contact information in your child's clothing or book backpack. File this information with each child's school.

KNOW WHO TO CALL AND WHERE TO GO

Make sure your children know who to call and where to meet in an emergency. Also teach them about dialing 911.

Contact name: _____

    Telephone (home, cell): _____

    Email address: _____

Out-of–state contact name: _____

    Telephone (home, cell): _____

    Email address: _____

Meeting place near home (phone #): _____

Secondary meeting place (include phone #): _____

Additional important phone numbers and information: _____

_____

FAMILY EMERGENCY COMMUNICATIONS NETWORK
FAMILY CALLING NETWORK

Some families, neighbors and churches have assigned people a short list of names to call in times of emergencies and developed plans to assist each other in times of crisis. If you do not have such a network in place, I recommend you start with your family, particularly if some family members are elderly, handicapped or a single parent.

Designate a family member to be responsible for developing and maintaining the family network connections. While this is for family members living in the same geographical area, it can also be used to develop a designated calling list to inform other family members who would be concerned following any major disaster. Make copies of the list of phone numbers and email addresses and designate who is responsible to contact whom. Share both cell and landline numbers. Share these copies with each family member.

FAMILY MESSAGING

With so many having smart phones, setting up group messaging between family members (or any group for that matter) has been greatly simplified. However, not everyone has smart phones and this easy method of communication may not be available to you.

Also, cellular communication may be interrupted for an indefinite period of time depending on the cause. Alternative communication plans need to be made and all family members made aware. Be sure to include information about alternative individuals to contact and/or institutions where family information can be left should one of the family members not be able to be reached for some reason during an emergency.

Consider getting your amateur radio operator license (ham radio operator) for emergency communication. For excellent radio equipment and information go to: www.tentec.com

FAMILY EMERGENCY COMMUNICATIONS NETWORK

Family Network Organizer: _____

Family members (local); phone numbers, email	Designated to Call
_____	_____
_____	_____
_____	_____
_____	_____
_____	_____
_____	_____

Family members (out of area); phone numbers, email	Designated to Call
_____	_____
_____	_____
_____	_____
_____	_____
_____	_____
_____	_____

NEIGHBORHOOD EMERGENCY COMMUNICATIONS NETWORK
NEIGHBORHOOD CALLING/MESSAGING NETWORK

Meet with your neighbors and discuss the possibility of setting up a neighborhood calling/messaging network for emergencies. If all neighbors do not have smart phones (so easy group messaging cannot be done), select one of the neighbors to develop and maintain the neighbor network connections. This could be a rotating responsibility. Keep up with neighbors that move into your neighborhood.

The Neighbor Network families may meet monthly or every two months to keep everyone up-to-date on preparedness activities. This will help build a sense of community. This can also be a time when the needs of a neighbor may come to light and everyone can "pitch-in" to help.

 See chapters 5 and 14 in *When All Plans Fail*.

NEIGHBORS' CONTACT INFORMATION

Even if you do not form a neighbor network, at least obtain contact information from your neighbors that are willing to and share your contact information with them.

NEIGHBORS' CONTACT INFORMATION

Landline phone number	Cell Phone	Email address
_____	_____	_____
_____	_____	_____
_____	_____	_____
_____	_____	_____

NEIGHBORHOOD EMERGENCY COMMUNICATIONS NETWORK

Neighbor Network Organizer: _____

Alternate Neighbor Network Organizer: _____

Neighbor's name; phone numbers, email   Designated to Call

_____   _____

_____   _____

_____   _____

_____   _____

_____   _____

_____   _____

_____   _____

_____   _____

_____   _____

_____   _____

NEIGHBORHOOD NETWORK MESSAGING

For all those in your Neighborhood Network with smart phones, set up group messaging to automate the process of getting messages out to the neighborhood.

LIVING WATER

"Worship the Lord your God, and his blessing will be on your food and water: I will take away sickness from among you."

Exodus 23: 24-25

PART THREE

HOPE

EMERGENCY SUPPLIES

OVERVIEW

IN PART THREE you will:

+ Gather your lists and copies of documents needed for emergencies.

+ Learn about water requirements, filtration and purification devices.

+ Learn about emergency food supplies and storage.

+ Learn tips on handling your medication needs for emergencies.

+ Find out what needs to go into a Barebones Emergency Kit.

+ Know what items go into your Personal Pouch if evacuation is needed.

+ Learn what items go into your Grab-and-Go bags at home, work and car, including a first aid kit and immunization records and recommendations.

+ Learn about important documents/records and how to prevent loss.

HOME EMERGENCY SUPPLIES
LONG TERM STORAGE AND GRAB-AND-GO BAGS

Emergency supplies need to be divided into long-term storage and your Grab-and-Go bags for the time when evacuation becomes necessary. Items for your car, workplace and pet Grab-and-Go bags are treated separately in the workbook. The emergency items for Home long term storage and family and personal Grab-and-Go bags are grouped as follows:

- Lists and documents needed.
- Water requirements/filtration/purification
- Food/cooking
- Medications
- General supplies
- Additional considerations for evacuation

In emergencies, having individual Grab-and-Go bags will make it much easier if families get separated or evacuate on foot rather than by a vehicle. This allows taking items for each person's unique needs.

For each item listed, I have used the designations below to indicate what is recommended for the Home long-term storage and Grab-and-Go supplies.

EMERGENCY ITEMS: LEVELS OF IMPORTANCE

H   Designates Home long term storage.

F   Designates Family Grab-and-Go bag filled with the items primarily intended for use by the whole family; like larger supply of food and water, cooking ware, fire extinguisher, etc.

P   Designates Personal Grab-and-Go bags for items each family member should carry in his or her own bag.

(***) Three asterisks indicate items I consider *essential*.

(**) Two asterisks for *general recommended* items.

(*)   One asterisk indicates *optional* items that often would make handling emergencies easier, but are not critical.

TIPS ON HOME EMERGENCY SUPPLIES

LONG TERM STORAGE AND GRAB-AND-GO BAGS

DON'T GET DISCOURAGED

Do not get discouraged by the long list. The basic essential items can be purchased or completed within a very few days and at minimal expense.

HOW MUCH TO PACK

Check the weight of your bag. A good rule of thumb is to not pack more than one-fourth of your body weight unless you are in good shape physically.

GRAB-AND-GO BAG STORAGE

Store your Grab-and-Go bag(s) where you have rapid and easy access. You may not have much time to get it in times of extreme emergency. Keep it stored away from high-risk areas such as the kitchen where fires are a greater potential risk

STORE WHAT YOU EAT, EAT WHAT YOU STORE

Gradually build up your home food supply to 3-6 months. While this seems daunting, remember food prices are going up. You will actually be saving $.

GETTING YOUR DOCUMENTS ON A USB FLASH DRIVE

If scanning documents and placing on USB flash drives is not something you are familiar with, have a family member or friend help you with this. There are commercial companies that provide this service for a small fee. Staples and Office Depot will scan documents for under 30 cents per page.

CASH ON HAND

If at all possible, keep at least $500 on hand in small bills for emergencies. You cannot be guaranteed access to your ATM or bank in some disasters.

LISTS AND DOCUMENTS NEEDED

While it is not possible to list everything needed for every individual, the lists will function as guidelines and jog your memory to include certain basic items. These decisions should not be made last minute. The **emergency contact list** and phone numbers and **family emergency contact list** you should have already compiled. Be sure to place in all needed locations.

RECENT INDIVIDUAL FAMILY MEMBER PICTURES

Having recent pictures of family members can be crucial in times of emergency to aid disaster relief workers and emergency personnel. Be sure to keep vital documents and pictures in water-proof containers. Digital pictures can be sent by the internet.

Take advantage of digital technology and place as much information on USB flash drives to make storage easier. For that matter, you could lay out documents and take close up pictures with a good digital camera for record keeping. This is not ideal, but it will work!

In addition to the **evacuation maps** and directions published by your community, be sure to include **maps** of your local area and/or places you might plan to go to if evacuating. In this section I have indicated to have these maps in your home and in the personal bags of the adult members of the family (in case the family gets separated). However, the maps are needed in each vehicle and at your workplace as well. This is stressed again in those sections of the workbook.

Consider having a GPS device other than one that may be in your vehicle if evacuation by foot is necessary. If the GPS in your car is detachable, take it with you if you have to evacuate by foot. Also, many of the newer phones have the option of having GPS service. Consider paying the extra for this benefit.

Having **physical copies of credit cards, personal identification and vital documents** is a good idea, but has greater risk of falling into the wrong hands. If this information is on a USB drive in your personal pouch, there is less chance of it being lost or stolen. Each responsible adult could have his or her own flash drive with individualized information.

LISTS AND DOCUMENTS NEEDED

Emergency contact list and phone numbers   HFP***

Family emergency contact list and phone numbers;   HFP***

Copies of important documents such as insurance   HFP***

Photocopies of identification (driver license etc.)   H P***

Photocopies of credit cards   H P***

Maps of local area and places you might evacuate to   H P***

          (See Appendix E in *When All Plans Fail*)

    H   Designates home long term storage
    F   Designates family Grab-and-Go bag
    P   Designates personal (each family member's Grab-and-Go bag)
    *** Designates essential item

KEEP DOCUMENTS SAFE

- Put documents and pictures in water proof containers in Grab-and-Go bags.

- Consider storing documents and pictures on USB flash drives and/or "in the cloud" on remote commercial servers.

- Consider storing documents outside your home (bank, family member, etc.)

WATER REQUIREMENTS/FILTRATION/PURIFICATION

SAFE DRINKING WATER IS TOP PRIORITY

Having sufficient safe water available per person is at the top of the list for essential health in times of crises.

Some type of **water filtration system** in your home for your drinking water is vital. There are many different types of home filtration systems, many of which are portable. The ability to both filter and purify water at home is very important. In some disasters you may be able to stay at home, but your normal water supply may be contaminated.

Some **portable water filtration** devices fit into purses or pockets. One company makes a small water filter that filters 50 gallons and with a small adapter for your water heater it makes this water available for drinking. I am stressing in this workbook the portable filtration devices, tablets or liquids that can be placed in a backpack or even in a purse or pocket to filter and/or purify water.

Most of the smaller water filters just filter the water and make the water from lakes, rivers, streams, rain water, etc. safe from giardia and cryptosporidia. In most cases this is sufficient.

WATER PURIFICATION

If water is contaminated by broken water lines, sewage or flooding, it is necessary to purify the water. The most efficient method of purification is boiling. Bringing water to a boil is sufficient. Both filtration and purification of water using tablets or liquids may be necessary if boiling is not an option. Visit the websites below.

www.princeton.edu/~oa/manual/water.shtml
www.generalecology.com/category/portable

WATER SUPPLY/FILTRATION/PURIFICATION ITEMS
FOR HOME AND GRAB-AND-GO BAGS

Water   HFP***
At home 1/2 to 1 gal/person/day needed
Recommend sufficient drinkable water in home for 14
days for each family member.

Water   FP***
3 day supply in containers next to Grab-and-Go Bags;
have small packets of water in Grab-and-Go bags; The
recommended 3 day supply may not be possible to carry if
evacuation is by foot

Home water filtration   H   ***
Either for entire home or only for drinking water.

Portable water filtration system   HFP***

Water purification   HFP***
Capability in addition to boiling (tablets or solution)

H   Designates home long term storage
F   Designates family Grab-and-Go bag
P   Designates personal (each family member's Grab-and-Go bag)
***   Designates essential item

 For water filtration and purification products visit:
www.aquamira.com

 For water purification information, reviews and comparisons.
www.waterfiltercomparisons.com

HOME EMERGENCY SUPPLIES

FOOD AND COOKING ITEMS

For your emergency food supply, choose foods that do not require refrigeration or special preparation. Select foods that require very little water or cooking. Avoid foods that will make you thirsty. To decide how much food to store, calculate the amount of food you need for two meals per person per day for 2 weeks. Be sure to include special dietary needs.

⚠️

STORE WHAT YOU EAT, EAT WHAT YOU STORE

Some people recommend 3-6 months of food storage. This gets to be very expensive for many families. Following the "Store what you eat and eat what you store" principle will allow you to achieve this goal little by little without breaking your monthly budget.

If some of the foods you choose to store are not normally part of your diet, begin to occasionally use these items and learn to prepare them.

Food storage: Unless the food you buy is already packaged in a long-term storage package, transfer food into food-grade containers with air-tight seals to protect from insects and rodents. Store food in a cool, dry area and away from gasoline or other fuels. Rotate emergency food stocks every 6 to 12 months. Some items can be stored indefinitely.

Alternative cooking sources in times of emergency include candle warmers and fondue pots. Charcoal grills and camp stoves are for outdoor use only. Campfire or fireplace cooking and solar cooking are also options.

Commercially **canned food** may be eaten out of the can without warming. If you heat the food in the can, wash the can thoroughly and remove any labels. Open the can before heating.

⚠️

Consider **planting a small garden** and/or have **garden seeds** for vegetables and other foods. Do not discuss information about your emergency food and water supply outside of your family.

FOOD AND COOKING ITEMS

FOR HOME AND GRAB-AND-GO BAGS

Essential food at home   H   ***
Recommend 3-6 months (minimum 2 weeks)
Particularly include special dietary foods if required

 See Appendix B in workbook or Appendix B
in *When All Plans Fail*

Food in Grab-and-Go bags   F P***
3 day food supply/person recommended
Include food for pets (pet Grab-and-Go bag)

Portable stove and stove fuel   F   **

Kitchen accessories and cooking utensils   F   **
Include manual can opener

Water proof matches   F P***

H   Designates home long term storage
F   Designates family Grab-and-Go bag
P   Designates personal (each family member's Grab-and-Go bag)
***   Designates essential item; ** recommended item; * optional item

 Camping guide to outdoor cooking and supplies:
www.lovetheoutdoors.com/camping/Outdoor_Cooking.htm
www.dutchovencookware.com

 Solar cooking:
www.solarcookers.org

 Purifying water while camping:
www.dummies.com/how-to/content/purifying-the-water-while-
camping.html

MEDICATIONS

Critical prescription medications often are very expensive and difficult to get more than one month's supply. At one time it was easier to get free samples through your doctor's office, but no longer. Insurance companies are clamping down on paying for expensive medications, forcing many patients to go to less costly alternatives, which may or not be equivalent.

Despite this, I encourage you to address this issue with your healthcare provider and try to get at least an extra month or two of medicines critical to your well-being. You may have to pay out of your own pocket to make this happen since insurance companies will not usually cover such expenses.

Having **written prescriptions for critical medications** is a good idea even if you have an extra month's supply at home and in your Grab-and-Go bag. Should you be separated from your meds and find yourself in a new location, you will at least be able to get a new prescription filled even before you are able to find another healthcare provider.

Discuss with your healthcare provider the possibility of having a general cache of **non-critical prescription medications** frequently used by household members to be available in times of crisis when it may be difficult to have access to your healthcare provider. You may have to fund this. Your healthcare provider will be able to guide you as to what medications would be advisable to store. *Keep written instructions with the medications.*

Over-the-counter medications are needed to be updated and kept at home and in all your Grab-and-Go bags. Have a first aid manual at home and in your family Grab-and-Go bag. Do not raid your first aid kits in your Grab-and-Go bags while at home. Use the home first aid kit.

PRESCRIPTION MEDICATIONS

For those individuals with prescription medicine, be sure to rotate regularly to not allow the medications to become outdated. Also, the written prescriptions should be renewed every 6 months for controlled substances and annually for non-controlled medications since many pharmacies will not honor older prescriptions.

MEDICATION

FOR HOME AND GRAB-AND-GO BAGS

Critical prescription medications   H P***
Recommend 1-2 months supply (beyond current month)
For example: diabetic and cardiovascular medications

Written prescriptions for critical medications   H P***

Non-critical prescription medications   HFP **
Include medications for pets (pet Grab-and-Go bag.)

Over-the-counter non-prescription medications   HFP **

Special dietary foods (can be as critical as medications)   HFP***
I have restated this here to denote how important this is.
Reminder: **Safe water is "medicine".**

H   Designates home long term storage
F   Designates family Grab-and-Go bag
P   Designates personal (each family member's Grab-and-Go bag)
***   Designates essential item; ** designates recommended item

The U.S Food and Drug Administration (FDA) has an excellent website for guidance about over-the-counter medications.

     www.fda.gov/buyonlineguide/WhatsRightForYou.htm

An excellent healthcare manual used around the world in primary healthcare settings and is useful to diagnose, treat and prevent common diseases is *Where There Is No Doctor*. If interested go to:

     www.hesperian.org/index.php

BAREBONES PERSONAL EMERGENCY KIT

Everyone should at least put together a barebones personal emergency kit. I recommend doing this immediately as you can then concentrate on getting the other emergency supplies for home, car and workplace. This simple list is within reach financially for everyone. Many of the items you already have in your home, just put them together as a kit.

Portable water filtration system   _____
Pocket size water filtration device to fit into purses or pockets. Typically these small water filters will filter 20-50 gallons and range in price from $10 to $30. One such filter has an adaptor to work with water heaters.

HOPE   www.aquamira.com

Water purification tablets or liquid   _____

Food, energy bars, trail mix   _____

Flashlight, small, waterproof   _____

Whistle   _____

First-aid kit, small   _____

Smoke hood   _____
(especially those living in high-rise or multi-storied buildings) Many types are available at widely varying costs.
HOPE   One website to visit:
         www.technonllc.com

Good walking shoes: (wear to work or have available)   _____

Cord (550 lb test; minimum 30feet)   _____

Extra money   _____

BAREBONES PERSONAL EMERGENCY KIT
ADDITIONAL BASIC PERSONAL EMERGENCY KIT ITEMS

The items listed below would not be allowed past airport security checks and federal buildings. At airports, if you have them on your person they will be taken from you unless you check them in your luggage. If airports and restricted public buildings are not an issue, the following basic personal emergency kit items are recommended for your barebones personal emergency kit, in addition to those listed on the facing page.

Multi-tool (e.g. Leatherman locking pliers)   _____

HOPE   www.multitool.org

Mini-pry bar (some are small enough to be key chains)   _____

HOPE   Unique pocket tools are intermittently available at:
www.atwoodknives.blogspot.com

Weather-proof matches   _____
(or matches in a water proof container)

EMT shears (bandage scissors)   _____

LIST OF PERSONAL POUCH DOCUMENTS/OTHER ITEMS

When evacuation becomes necessary and you have put your grab-and-go bags in your car, I recommend you put most of your money and the essential identification documents in a special **personal pouch** to be carried on your person at all times. This applies to each adult and older child in your family that will be using a personal pouch. This greatly reduces the risk of loss or theft of these vital documents. Also, these personal vital documents stay with individual family members should you become separated in an emergency situation. Each family member will have some cash as well.

PERSONAL POUCH WORN UNDER CLOTHING

The personal pouch is worn under clothing to make it less conspicuous and so it will not easily become separated from you during disasters. I don't recommend using "fanny packs" which can easily be separated from your body by theft or mishap when you are in the middle of a disaster.

 One website for personal travel pouches is:
www.nextag.com/money-pouch-travel/products-html

 (Chapter 6, Put You Own Mask On First in *When All Plans Fail.*)

These personal pouch documents are extremely sensitive. If each adult or older child stores them in their personal Grab-and-Go bag, they need to be in water proof containers (preferably lockable). Place the water proof container with the documents in a pocket that can be locked or in a hidden pocket. Transfer these documents to the personal pouches after evacuating.

Put enough cash in the Family Grab-and-Go bag for several days. Do not put all of your emergency money in one place. Having some divided between the adults and older children in their personal pouches would be wise. Keep the money in the water proof container with the passport and social security cards. Each family member should transfer the money they are responsible for to his or her pouch after evacuating.

LIST OF PERSONAL POUCH DOCUMENTS/OTHER ITEMS

Passport _____

Social Security Card(s) for self, family. _____
Adults and older teenagers should carry them in their own
personal pouch.

Driver's license _____
(I am assuming you will already have this with you and
suggest you place this in your pouch when you evacuate.)

Bank cards and /or credit cards _____
(I am assuming you will already have these with you and
suggest you place them in the pouch when you evacuate.)

Money _____
(place some extra cash in the Family Grab-and-Go bag)

List of immunizations with dates for each family member. _____
Have copy of each family member's individual
immunization records in his or her Grab-and-Go bag
(and USB flash drive).

Medical alert information (also wear tag or wrist band) _____

List of family contact information _____
(phone, email addresses, etc.) Include pictures of family
members.

Emergency contact list _____

Extra set of car and house keys _____

Prepaid phone cards _____
If your cell phones are not working and you are away from
home, prepaid phone cards can be used from any working
phone.

USB flash drives _____
Copies of your important documents, pictures of family,
to be carried by all family members.

GENERAL EMERGENCY SUPPLIES

FOR HOME AND GRAB-AND-GO BAGS

Portable, battery powered radio/TV   HF   ***
With extra batteries or hand rechargeable radio.
As a precaution, have a second radio.   P   *

Flashlights and extra batteries   HFP***
or flashlights that don't require batteries or solar
powered.

First aid kit and first aid manual   HFP***

Insect repellent (consider mosquito netting)   HFP***

Smoke hoods   H P***
(especially those living in high-rise or multi-storied buildings I would list this as triple asterisks (***))

    www.technonllc.com or www.smokemask.org

Flame resistant poncho   H P   *
Those living in high-rise or multi-storied buildings list
this as **.

          Visit www.technonllc.com .

Fire extinguisher (ABC type)   HF   ***
There are small aerosolized can fire extinguishers that
easily fit in a Grab-and-Go bag and/or your car.
Aerosolized can fire extinguisher demo on You Tube.

          www.youtube.com/watch?v=ofO7pIksJSg. Also visit:
          www.firstalert.com/tundra_fire_extinguishing_spray.php

H   Designates home long term storage
F   Designates family Grab-and-Go bag
P   Designates personal (each family member's Grab-and-Go bag)
***   Designates essential item; ** recommended item; * optional item

GENERAL EMERGENCY SUPPLIES

FOR HOME AND GRAB-AND-GO BAGS

Whistle   HFP***

Emergency blanket (space blanket)   HF ***
These blankets are very thin, light weight and help protect
from wind chill, radiant heat loss and evaporative heat
loss. Use a regular blanket outside the emergency blanket
if lying on a cold surface. Cost is only $2 to $4. Every
family member should carry one.

> www.nitro-pak.com/product_info.php?
> products_id=216

Crowbar (small)   HF   **

> Unique pocket tools intermittently available at:
> www.atwoodknives.blogspot.com.

Small tool kit (wrench, pliers, multi tools)   FP **

> www.multitool.org

Roll of duct tape (flattened)   F   **

Nylon cord (550-lb. test)   F   **

Heavy duty plastic garbage bags   F   **

Signal flare   F   **
For Grab-and-Go bags I particularly would recommend
NOT using incendiary flares. There are very good, rela-
tively inexpensive flares available that are battery operated.
See the following website:

> www.ingramproducts.com

Sanitation and hygiene items   P **

GENERAL EMERGENCY SUPPLIES
FOR HOME AND GRAB-AND-GO BAGS

Extra set of house keys and car keys ⎯⎯⎯⎯ F P ***

Needle and thread (sewing kit) ⎯⎯⎯⎯ F P **

Small aerosol canister fire extinguisher ⎯⎯⎯⎯ F ***

Scissors
(preferably EMT scissors, also called bandage scissors) ⎯⎯⎯⎯ F **

Plastic sheeting ⎯⎯⎯⎯ F **

Medium size plastic bucket with tight lid ⎯⎯⎯⎯ F **
Only practical if you evacuate by car.

Disinfectant and household chlorine bleach ⎯⎯⎯⎯ F **

Small shovel (foldable) ⎯⎯⎯⎯ F **

Tube tent ⎯⎯⎯⎯ F **

Compass ⎯⎯⎯⎯ F **

Work gloves ⎯⎯⎯⎯ F **

Sturdy shoes, hiking boots ⎯⎯⎯⎯ P **

Sleeping bag or blanket (per person) ⎯⎯⎯⎯ P **

H   Designates home long term storage
F   Designates family Grab-and-Go bag
P   Designates personal (each family member's Grab-and-Go bag)
***   Designates essential item; ** recommended item; * optional item

44

GENERAL EMERGENCY SUPPLIES

FOR HOME AND GRAB-AND-GO BAGS

Extra clothing   P **
Recommended clothing will vary according to where you
live

Clothing for cold climate:
 * Jacket / coat, least bulky providing adequate warmth   P **
 * Long pants, long-underwear, long sleeve shirt   P **
 * Hat / head covering / gloves / scarf   P **

Rain gear   P ***

Eye glasses   P ***
(if applicable), contact lens (extra) and contact lens
solution (be sure to renew regularly)

Goggles   P **
(can use simple swimming goggles) for eye protection

Hearing aid batteries (if applicable)   P ***

Items for infants   P ***
(formula, diapers, bottles pacifiers, etc. Make sure the for-
mula is renewed regularly).

Paper, pens, pencils (water proof container)   P **
Waterproof notebooks maybe found at sporting goods stores.

Grab-and-Go bag for pets   P E T***
(pet care covered in separate section)

FIRST AID KIT

There are two good publications to back up your knowledge of first aid. The first is the Red Cross first aid manual (available at Red Cross) and the second is Where *There Is No doctor, A Village Health Care Handbook*. The Hesperian organization also publishes a book entitled *"Where There is No Dentist."*

 www.hesperian.org to obtain a copy.

You need first aid kits in all the following Grab-and-Go bags:
* Family (most complete kit for use by the entire family)
* Personal
* Workplace
* Car
* Pets

All the items listed for the first aid kit are for the more complete first aid kit to be placed in the family Grab-and-Go bag. Each individual family member should pick and choose from the list the items to place in his or her own personal first aid kit. Determine what you want in your car and workplace first aid kits.

POISON INGESTION RX:
Keep instructions in all first aid kits should someone be poisoned:

syrup of ipecac (use only if advised by a Poison Center) _____

activated charcoal (use only if advised by a Poison Center) _____

 National Capital Poison Center   1-800-222-1222

 www.poison.org

National Battery Ingestion Hotline   1-202-625-3333
(may call collect)

SPECIAL HANDLING OF FIRST AID KITS

I recommend that you seal your medication and first aid containers. You may use tape, wire or string and place a tag on it showing the date the contents need to be updated. This is an important safety measure that professional emergency teams do. Emergency kits are closed with some type of seal that must be broken to access the supplies. Whenever the seal is broken you will know that the contents need to be reviewed and any missing items need to be replaced. If the seal is intact, then the right supplies are in the bag! Keep a list of what you keep in each first aid kit inside the kit to remind you of what should be there if the seal is broken.

FIRST AID KIT

Band-Aids (many assorted sizes) _____

Antiseptic / alcohol wipes _____

Hand sanitizer bottles (2) _____

Topical antibiotic ointment _____

Topical hydrocortisone cream _____

Hydrogen peroxide _____

Petroleum jelly (tube) _____

Sunscreen _____

Thermometer _____

FIRST AID KIT

Lighter _____

Latex gloves (several pairs) _____

Sterile gauze pads, 2-inch (10) _____

Sterile gauze pads, 4- inch (10) _____

Sterile roller bandages, 2-inch (5) _____

Sterile roller bandages, 4-inch (5) _____

Sterile cotton balls (small pack) _____

Adhesive bandage tape, hypoallergenic; 1 inch _____

Triangular bandages (3) _____

Bandage scissors (EMT scissors) _____

Maxi sanitary napkins (5) (for major wounds) _____

Irrigating syringe _____

Ace bandages 2-inch, 3-inch and 4 –inch (2 each size) _____

Two **tweezers** (one regular size, one small) _____

Needle (consider including suture material and set) _____

Scalpel with extra blades _____

Bismuth subsalicylate (Pepto-Bismol) _____
Check with your doctor for children's dosage.

FIRST AID KIT

Antacids   _____

Pain relievers
(non-aspirin pain relievers such as acetaminophen, ibuprofen) _____

Stool softeners _____

Antifungal ointment/cream (e.g. miconazole) _____

Cough and cold medications (OTC) _____

Visine eye drops _____

Contact lens wearers: extra pair, solution _____

Diphenhyramine (Benadryl) _____
This is an antihistamine used for hives, allergic rhinitis, etc. Check with your doctor for children's dosages

Epi-Pen for severe allergic reactions (insects, food) _____

HOPE   www.epipen.com (requires prescription)

Ophthalmic antibiotic (This will require a prescription.) _____

CRITICAL MEDICATIONS KEPT SEPARATE

Critical prescription medications are kept in each family member's Grab-and-Go bag separate from his or her first aid kit because the kit may be used for other people and you do not want to be separated from your critical meds!

GENERAL EMERGENCY SUPPLIES
ADDITIONAL CONSIDERATIONS FOR EVACUATION

PERSONAL POUCH

Each adult and child old enough to be responsible for personal identification documents and money should have his or her individual personal pouch pre-filled and included in their own personal Grab-and-Go bag. Items such as drivers license and extra money can be added to the pouch while evacuation is taking place. See the section on your Personal Pouch for list of what should be included. This pouch is to be worn under clothing to not attract attention.

ALTERNATIVE EMERGENCY TRANSPORTATION

Consideration for using bicycles, motorcycles or mopeds would be for those rare instances when evacuation was not possible by car or a larger motorized means of transportation. For those without a vehicle, prior transportation arrangements should have already been made. If you or a family member is elderly, handicapped or does not have a vehicle, then make sure appropriate transportation planning has been worked out.

SELF-DEFENSE EQUIPMENT

In my book *When All Plans Fail* I cover this topic briefly. This is an area of personal choice. The area of firearms and martial arts are specialized areas I feel I can give only limited recommendations. For those not wanting to use firearms, an alternative is the use of pepper spray with a SHU (Scoville Heat Unit) number of at least 2 million.

www.mace.com or www.zarc.com .

AIR PURIFYING RESPIRATORS (GAS MASKS)

There are many different types of air purifying respirators (gas masks) for chemical, biological, radiological and nuclear hazards. Visit the websites:

www.approvedgasmasks.com or www.airgas.com

GENERAL EMERGENCY SUPPLIES
ADDITIONAL CONSIDERATIONS FOR EVACUATION

FIRE ESCAPE LADDER

For those living in a residence or apartment with more than one floor, determine escape routes to determine if a fire escape ladder is necessary. A good website for several fire escape ladder options is:

 www.fireescapesystems.com/products.asp.

INFLATABLE RAFT

If you live in an area at risk for flooding, consider obtaining an inflatable raft if you do not already have a boat at home. A raft will take up less storage space and is more economical. Sizes and prices vary widely. This could be neighborhood project to lower the expense.

 www.inflatablerafts.com.

KITTY LITTER AND CHLOROPHYLL TABLETS

If one has to evacuate by vehicle, it may not be practical to stop roadside for toilet breaks. This would particularly be true for children and elderly family members who are non-ambulatory. Kitty litter in a bucket will absorb liquid and dry up stools. Give chlorophyll tablets to an incontinent individual to reduce fecal smells (get 200 tablets for less than $10).

SAFETY HELMET

There are several natural hazards where a safety helmet would be useful. If you anticipate being involved in relief efforts consider getting a safety helmet. Sports helmets could fulfill this role as an alternative.

GRAB-AND-GO BAG FOR PET(S)

Handling pets in emergencies is covered in a separate section. Pet supplies should be kept with the family Grab-and-Go bags. Also, don't forget to have the extra supplies of pet food for long-term storage.

IMPORTANT DOCUMENT STORAGE

ORIGINAL DOCUMENTS

Original documents of important papers need to be stored in a safe/lockbox at home that is water and fire proof or else need to be stored off-site in a place such as a bank safe deposit box. Exceptions would be the personal identification documents that you either carry on your person most of the time or need frequent access to. Copies of these documents need to be placed in the safe/lockbox or bank safe deposit box. Digital storage of important documents on flash drives in addition to physical copies is discussed several times in the work book. **Password protect digital information.**

Suggestions where copies of documents should be stored indicated by:
  S Designates a safe/lockbox at home.
  B Designates bank safe deposit box/law office/executor of estate
  P Designates personal Grab-and-Go bag or personal pouch
  W Designates workplace Grab-and-Go bag
  F Designates family Grab-and-Go bag
  C Designates car Grab-and-Go bag

Personal Identification Documents
  Driver's license original or photo ID card   S P
  Passport or naturalization papers   S P W
  Social security card   S P
  Birth certificate (certified with original seal) S P

Medical Records   S P
(each family member; include immunizations)

Deeds and titles to real estate   S B

Titles to vehicles; registrations in safe/lockbox   S B

Credit cards: S B F
photocopies of both sides; include recent statement

IMPORTANT DOCUMENT STORAGE

Insurance Policies

Life Insurance:	S P
Home owners/renters insurance:	S F
Flood insurance if needed:	S F
Earthquake insurance if needed:	S F
Health insurance policy (policy ID in wallet, purse)	S F
Disability insurance policy:	S F
Vehicular insurance policies:	S F C

Documentation of Investments / Trusts

Stock/bond certificates	S B
Trust documents	S B

Documentation of Debts

Loan papers: mortgage (most recent statement), other real estate	S B
Auto loan papers / monthly statement, other vehicular loans	S B

WILLS, LIVING WILLS, POWER OF ATTORNEY, ETC.

Wills, Living wills (law firm will have copy if drawn up by them)	S B F
Power-of attorney	S B F
Marriage certificate (or divorce decree)	S B F

Give a copy of your will/ living will or trust to the individual or lawyer or institution that is designated as the executor of your will or trust. Keep an extra key for the bank deposit box in your personal pouch.

SAFEGUARD YOUR BUSINESS RECORDS

Making digital backups of client contact information, payroll records, accounts receivable and accounts payable are the most essential pieces of information you will need for a quick start up of your business following a disaster. Backups online as well as on flash drives would be prudent.

IMMUNIZATION RECORDS AND RECOMMENDATIONS

Having records of immunizations is usually not a problem for school age children due to school requirements for immunizations. Adult records are often more difficult to locate and may even be lost. The Center for Disease Control (CDC) has published emergency preparedness guidelines and recommendations following a disaster(see website below).

 http://emergency.cdc.gov/disasters/disease/vaccrecdisplaced.asp

The purpose of these CDC recommendations is to protect people of all ages against vaccine-preventable diseases in accordance with current recommendations and to reduce the likelihood of outbreaks of vaccine-preventable diseases in large crowded group settings. Be sure your family's immunizations are up-to-date!

CDC recommends the following vaccines should be given to evacuees living in crowded group settings, unless the person has written documentation of having already received them:

+ Influenza: everyone 6 months of age or older should receive influenza vaccine. Children 8 years old or younger should receive 2 doses, at least one month apart, unless they have a documented record of a previous dose of influenza vaccine, in which case they should receive 1dose.
+ Varicella: everyone 12 months of age or older should receive one dose of this vaccine unless they have a reliable history of chickenpox or a documented record of immunization.
+ MMR: everyone 12 months of age or older and born during or after 1957 should receive one dose of this vaccine unless they have a documented record of 2 doses of MMR.

I personally recommend Hepatitis B vaccine (HepB). CDC recommends this for all disaster responders.

IMMUNIZATION RECORDS AND RECOMMENDATIONS

IMMUNIZATION GUIDELINES WITHOUT RECORDS

CDC guidelines for immunizations to be offered to individuals who do not have immunization records is given below.

Children 10 and younger: should be treated as if they were up-to-date for their age (unless parental report indicates otherwise) and be given age appropriate immunizations not yet received. This includes the following:

- Diphtheria and tetanus toxoids and acellular pertussis vaccine (DTaP)
- Inactivated Poliovirus vaccine (IPV)
- *Haemophilus influenzae* type b vaccine (Hib)
- Hepatitis B vaccine (HepB)
- Pneumococcal conjugate vaccine (PCV)
- Measles-mumps-rubella vaccine (MMR)
- Varicella vaccine unless reliable history of chickenpox
- Influenza vaccine for all children 6-59 months of age, and 6 months through 10 years of age with an underlying medical condition.
- Hepatitis A vaccination is recommended 1 year of age and older
- Rotavirus vaccine

Children/adolescents 11-18 years of age:

- Adult tetanus/diphtheria toxoids/acellular pertussis vaccine (Tdap)
- Meningococcal conjugate vaccine (MCV) (11-12 and 15 years only)
- Influenza vaccine for all children 6-59 months of age, and children 6 months through 10 years of age with an underlying medical condition

Adult immunization recommendations:

- Adult formulation tetanus and diphtheria toxoids (Td) if 10 years or more since receipt of any tetanus toxoid-containing vaccine.
- Pneumococcal polysaccharide vaccine (PPV) for adults 65 years of age or older or with a high risk condition
- Influenza vaccine

WORKPLACE PLANS

Mark the following items related to disaster planning in your workplace:

My workplace has a written disaster plan.   Yes No

    I have a copy.   Yes No

My workplace has a building evacuation plan.   Yes No

    The building evacuation plan is regularly practiced. Yes No

The heating, ventilation and air conditioning systems are   Yes No
secure and have good filtering.

I know how to turn off critical electric equipment   Yes No
(such as air conditioning) if needed.

My workplace has a first aid kit that is updated regularly   Yes No
And has good-date medications and supplies.

My workplace has a portable, battery-operated radio and   Yes No
extra batteries.

My workplace has hard hats and masks for dust.   Yes No

My guess is that many smaller businesses do not have many of the items listed above. If not, take the initiative and help your office prepare for emergencies.

WORKPLACE EMERGENCY SUPPLIES KIT

Personal first aid kit (separate from workplace first aid kit) _____

Prescription medications at work. Rotate monthly. _____

Comfortable walking shoes or boots (if evacuation by foot) _____

Emergency food (energy bars, trail mix; rotate periodically) _____

Emergency water (2-3 16oz. bottles, rotate periodically; consider having a pocket-size water filtration system) _____

Flashlight (type that does not require batteries) _____

Small emergency radio (batteries/wind-up/solar _____

Mini-pry bar _____

Smoke hood in case of fire _____

Extra keys (home and vehicles) _____

Duct tape (small flattened roll) _____

Nylon cord (550-lb test if you work in multi-story building) _____

Rain gear (such as poncho, compact umbrella) _____

Copies of ID, drivers license, passport, etc. _____

Put items in a readily accessible Grab-and-Go bag. Maintain your emergency kit, particularly the food, first aid kit and medications. Periodically review your situation and modify contents of kit accordingly.

CHECKLIST FOR CAR EMERGENCY SUPPLIES

Jumper cables (15-20 feet long)   _____ ***
6-gauge wire cables will work for most cars and SUV's, but I prefer 4-gauge wire cables. This will work not only for your vehicle, but if you have to help someone with a larger vehicle.

Battery charger   _____ **
I have come across a neat battery charger system that works through your cigarette lighter socket. You don't have to get out of your car and it has about a 5 year life.

    HOPE   www.porta-jump.com (approximately $30.00) or Photovoltaic trickle battery charger

Flares   _____ ***
Having an emergency alerting system is essential particularly in bad weather or at night. I prefer non-incendiary flares.

    HOPE   www.ingramproducts.com/
www.superbrightleds.com/moreinfo/emergency-strobe/9-in-1-super-bright-led-safety-flare/1317/

Flat tire inflation canister (non-explosive)   _____ ***

Spare tire and jack   _____ ***

Small tool kit   _____ ***

DESIGNATE ONE VEHICLE FOR EVACUATION

If you have more than one vehicle, you should designate one vehicle for evacuation. Put the greater amount of emergency supplies in it.

(***) Three asterisks indicate items that should be in all your vehicles.
(**) Two asterisks for extra items for designated evacuation vehicle.
(*) One asterisk is for optional items (handy but not critical.)

CHECKLIST FOR CAR EMERGENCY SUPPLIES

Water: frequently rotate supply (1-2 gallons)   _____   ***

High energy foods / power bars/ trail mix   _____   ***

First aid supplies (more complete in evacuation vehicle) _____   ***

Flashlight / batteries / or does not need batteries   _____   ***

Road maps   _____   ***
(consider GPS system if not in your car already)

Cell phone charger left in car at all times   _____   ***

Emergency blankets (space blanket / regular blanket)   _____   ***

Ice scrapper (if applicable)   _____   ***

Backpack to store car emergency supplies   _____   ***

Umbrella, rain gear   _____   ***

Emergency radio, battery operated / hand-rechargeable _____   **

Fire extinguisher, small aerosolized can   _____   **

Antifreeze, can of oil   _____   **

Small shovel, foldable   _____   **

Extra pair of shoes, work gloves   _____   *

Towing line or chain   _____   *

Sleeping bag(s)   _____   *
     HOPE   (Consider Bivy Sacks-small/compact ($30.)
         www.campmor.com/outdoor/gear/
         Prouct89033?CS_003=2477120&CS_010=89033

DESTINATION KNOWN

"I'm the Way and the Truth and the Life
No one comes to the Father
except through me."

John 14:6

HOPE
EVACUATION READINESS

OVERVIEW

IN PART FOUR you will:

+ Obtain your local community's evacuation plans.

+ Make two evacuation plans of your own, one primary and an alternate.

+ Consider getting a GPS (Global Positioning System).

+ Make a checklist of what to do before evacuating your home.

+ Learn about shutting off electricity, gas and water utilities in your home.

+ Learn how to prepare for evacuating high-rise buildings.

+ Make a checklist of what to have and do in case of fire in your home.

+ Learn about emergency care for family members with special needs.

+ Learn about planning pet care in emergencies.

EVACUATION PLANS

DISASTERS THAT MAY REQUIRE EVACUATION

Home fires, floods, hurricanes, tornadoes, wildfires, mudslides, earthquakes, loss of electrical power, volcanoes, tsunamis, radiation threats, chemical threats, and terrorist threats are among the various natural and man-made hazards that may make evacuation from your home necessary.

EVACUATION AT A MOMENTS NOTICE

Some of these hazards give adequate time to prepare for evacuation and others require being ready at a moments notice. That's why pre-planning and having Grab-and-Go bags is so vital!

Communities that have experienced natural disasters that required mass evacuation have published evacuation plans pre-determined by local authorities. Many places have road signs designating evacuation routes.

While it is best to follow established evacuation routes recommended by authorities, watching people trying to escape from Katrina on clogged freeways and then running out of gas only re-enforces the need to have contingency plans. Plan at least two alternate evacuation routes. Include detailed maps and directions. Keep copies in all your vehicles.

GPS SYSTEMS (GLOBAL POSITIONING SYSTEMS)

Emergency radio broadcasts will alert you to any traffic conditions or alternative recommended routes. Many people have GPS systems and these can be extremely helpful if you have to take unfamiliar routes. Cell phone companies offer GPS service.

Remember: for traveler information dial 511 or www.511.com

WHAT TO DO BEFORE EVACUATING YOUR HOME

The checklist is based on the assumption you will have at least a few minutes, hours and at times days to get ready for evacuation. Evacuate early enough to avoid severe weather and traffic tie-ups. For a few disasters there will be no time and the only thing you and your family will be able to do is hopefully grab your Grab-and-Go bags on your way out the door and get in your vehicle and leave your home.

KEEP GAS TANK AT LEAST HALF-FILLED

Getting into the habit of keeping your gas tank at least half-filled at all times will make sure you are able to evacuate on short notice.

Place this checklist in your personal notebook and post in a place where family members will be able to periodically review such as where you have placed your Grab-and-Go bags.

CRITICAL NOTE: PRE-ARRANGE TRANSPORTATION

If you are elderly, handicapped or do not have your own transportation, *pre-arrange transportation* with family, friends, neighbors or emergency services. Have a back-up plan in place.

Churches can play a significant role in helping coordinate such transportation services.

EVACUATION PLANS

(Check When Done)

1. I have obtained local evacuation plans.   _____

2. I have made alternate evacuations plans.   _____

3. I have copies of the local and alternative evacuation   _____
   plans in

   * my notebook   _____

   * my Grab-and-Go bags (family, car and work)   _____
     Indicate in the front of your notebook where your
     Grab-and-Go bags are stored

   * my workplace   _____

4. I have identified **where family members should meet**   _____
   if the family is separated when a disaster hits.

   Safe site near home

   _____

   Secondary site some distance from home

   _____

   Person to contact (home and cell phone numbers) if family
   communication plans cannot be followed. Don't forget 911.

   _____

CHECKLIST FOR EVACUATION OF YOUR HOME

1. Gather your family from schools and workplaces if possible. Depending on the emergency, it may be necessary to meet at a pre-designated site or for each family member to remain at school or the workplace and follow emergency procedures there.

2. Unplug electrical equipment such as radios, televisions and small appliances (except freezers and refrigerators unless flooding is expected).

OR

3. If it is advisable to turn off all utilities, turn off all individual electrical circuits before shutting off the main circuit breaker.

4. Shut off the main water valve to your home.

5. Shut off the natural gas to your home.

6. Put on your personal pouch worn under clothing. Ideally, this should be pre-packed except for those items you use everyday and would most likely already be on your person. Have a list in your pouch of items that need to be included at the last minute. Don't forget your cash in small bills!

7. Securely lock all doors and windows.

8. Put your Grab-and-Go bag(s) in your car. Take only one car if possible. Have your evacuation routes handy.

9. Leave a note in a conspicuous place indicating where you plan to go and how you can be reached.

10. As soon as practical, let others know where you have re-located.

SHUTTING OFF ELECTRICITY, GAS AND WATER UTILITIES

Take the time to go through the checklists below to make sure everyone in the family that needs to know will be prepared to shut off the utilities.

Electricity Shut Off Checklist
- I know where my electricity circuit box is located.　　Yes　No
  Location:

- I know how to shut off electricity to the entire house.　　Yes　No

- I have taught all responsible household members　　Yes　No
  how to shut off electricity to the whole house.

HOW TO SAFELY SHUT OFF CIRCUIT BREAKERS

For your safety, shut off all individual circuits before shutting off the main circuit breaker!

Gas Shut Off Checklist
- I have contacted my local gas company　　Yes　No
  and know how to properly shut off all gas appliances
  and gas service to my home.
  Location: _____

- I have taught all responsible household members　　Yes　No
  how to properly shut off all gas appliances and services.

Water Shut Off Checklist
- I know where the main water valve to my home is　　Yes　No
  located and I know how to shut it off.
  Location: _____

- I have taught all responsible household members　　Yes　No
  how to properly shut off the main water valve.

EVACUATION CHECKLIST FOR HIGH-RISE BUILDINGS

Many individuals living in high rise buildings may not have an automobile and rely on public transportation. If this is your situation, you will still need to follow both CHECKLISTS FOR EVACUATION OF YOUR HOME and HIGH RISE BUILDINGS.

 See chapter 5 in *When All Plans Fail*.

CHECKLIST FOR EVACUATING A HIGH-RISE BUILDING

I know the locations of every exit in my building. _____

No building exits are blocked or locked. _____

I have planned my escape route(s) in case of fire. _____

My building conducts fire drills. _____

I have reported any fire hazards to the fire department. _____

I have a flashlight (high-powered, non-incendive). _____

I have smoke escape hoods for each family member. _____

All of my family knows how to use the hoods. _____

I have an escape ladder in my living quarters (if needed). _____

My building has an emergency light system. _____

Building elevators have pry bars to open jammed doors. _____

All exits have an emergency pry bar, axe, and claw tool. _____

All building exits have ABC fire extinguishers. _____

CHECKLIST FOR FIRES IN THE HOME

SMOKE DETECTORS AND CARBON MONOXIDE MONITORS

Fires starting inside the home are a universal risk. To prepare for such events, smoke detectors and carbon monoxide monitors are a must. Using battery operated smoke detectors is important. Have at least one fire extinguisher of the ABC type. Teach your family members how to use it.

ESCAPE ROUTES FOR FIRES

Planning escape routes and practicing with your children, handicapped and elderly family members is very crucial. Having escape routes pre-planned will lessen confusion even for the average adult.

Draw a floor plan of your home and mark two routes of escape from each room. Post a copy of these plans in each child's room at eye level. Practice the escape routes with children. Make it into a game!

ESCAPE LADDERS

If you have 2 or more stories in your home, consider the possible need for an escape ladder. Determine which ladder is best suited for you. Even in a high-rise situation, a ladder may allow you to escape to a lower floor.

FAMILY MEETING PLACE

Establish a place to meet should the family need to evacuate the home. Identify a place near your home and one place outside the immediate area of the home. Having a pre-determined place to meet will lessen anxiety of not knowing where to meet up with your family.

DOCUMENTATION OF PERSONAL PROPERTY

Another aspect of disaster planning that applies to all hazards that might destroy your personal property is having adequate documentation of your personal property. The easiest way to document your property is to take photos or videos of the interior and exterior of your home. Be sure to include your personal belongings that may not be readily visible when you take your video or photos. Supporting documents of major purchases is also helpful.

CHECKLIST OF ITEMS NEEDED IN CASE OF
FIRES IN THE HOME

Smoke detectors: adequate number in good working order _____
(battery operated)placed strategically (bedrooms, kitchen, rooms with fireplace)

Carbon monoxide detectors: _____
may be part of smoke detectors

Fire extinguishers: (ABC type, placed in or near kitchen, _____
rooms with fireplaces; small aerosolized can fire extinguishers handy in bedrooms and easy for older children to use)

    HOPE www.firstalertstore.com/store/ catalog.asp?item=1209

Smoke hoods: (especially if living in multi-storied buildings)_____

    HOPE www.technonllc.com

Flame resistant poncho: (if living in multi-storied buildings) _____

    HOPE www.technonllc.com .

Emergency escape ladder(s): _____
For those living in a residence or apartment with more than one floor, determine if a fire escape ladder is necessary. For several fire escape ladder options visit:

    HOPE www.fireescapesystems.com

Take photos or video your home, inside and outside _____
For insurance purposes in case of fire. Keep copies off-site.

    HOPE www.ready.gov/home-fires

CARING FOR FAMILY MEMBERS WITH SPECIAL NEEDS

It requires careful advanced planning to assist family members with special needs during emergencies. Careful planning is needed to safely care for the elderly, the handicapped (including deaf and blind), small children, those with special medical conditions, illnesses (including mental illness) or nutritional requirements. In addition, special assistance may be needed by non-English speaking family members.

Choose the care giving location of a special needs family member carefully. If possible, pre-position the family member in a place in the home where moving would not be required if a disaster threatened.

EVACUATION OF SPECIAL NEEDS FAMILY MEMBERS

+ If you or a family member is without personal transportation, address these disaster preparation issues with your family, neighbors, church, healthcare givers and your local fire and rescue unit first responders.
+ Pack routine and special need items specifically required for elderly and handicapped family members.
+ It will often require two people to assist the very elderly or physically handicapped individuals to move them to a safe place or to an appropriate vehicle. This is part of pre-disaster planning.
+ A back-up evacuation transportation plan must be in place.
+ Accommodating an elderly or handicapped individual and all the equipment needed for them may take up more space than you realize. Do a "test run" to make sure. If eliminating some desired medical equipment that is not absolutely necessary allows you to take only one vehicle, I'd recommend that.
+ It is critical to have portable medical equipment such as portable oxygen or battery powered nebulizers if that is a requirement. You cannot be scrambling for this equipment at the last minute.

Chapter 7 Bridge Over Troubled Waters: People With Special Needs, in *When All Plans Fail*

CARING FOR FAMILY MEMBERS WITH SPECIAL NEEDS DURING EMERGENCIES

Alerting Deaf and Blind Individuals: obtain a vibrating beeper to alert the deaf individual of emergencies and audio alerts for the blind.

 www.deaf-alerter.com/index.php or
www.americanmedicalalarms.com or
www.nws.noaa.gov/nwr/info/special_needs.html

Elderly and Handicapped Living Alone
Many emergency alert systems are available for the elderly whether living alone or with family. Two sites are listed below.

 www.babyboomercaretaker.com/senior-care/Emergency-Alert-For-Elderly.html or www.americanmedicalalarms.com/

Evacuation transportation: Reliance on a specialized transportation service that provides care for many special needs individuals may not be available if a major disaster strikes.

Evacuation Route for Those With Special Needs: Plan a route that avoids staircases, hills or rough terrain if any portion of the route needs to be done by foot. If this is impossible, the need for early evacuation for even potential disasters becomes paramount.

Flood Emergencies: If flooding is a risk where you have family members with special needs, it is highly recommended to evacuate your home well in advance even if it is not certain evacuation is absolutely necessary.

Pre-package Medications: Make sure medications needed for the special needs family member(s) are pre-packaged and part of his or her Grab-and-Go bag. Update the list of needed meds rotate on a regular basis. Keep at least one month's supply.

Diabetics On Insulin: Planning will include a means of keeping insulin supplies at a cool temperature if refrigeration facilities are not available.

 www.frio.com.cn/english/comments.asp

PLANNING PET AND ANIMAL CARE IN ENERGENCIES

Write out your emergency care plan for your pet.   _____
Good advice and guidelines for disaster planning for pets is
available at the websites below:

          www.ready.gov/caring-animals
www.bt.cdc.gov/disasters/petprotect.asp

Make sure your pet has proper ID   _____

Keep veterinarian records and vaccinations up-to-date   _____
 and pack in pet Grab-and-Go bag
(if pet is to evacuate with the family)

Obtain a pet carrier and leash if you don't have   _____

Pack pet Grab-and-Go bag   _____
(if pet is to evacuate with the family

Find out which hotels or emergency shelters allow pets   _____
or where pet shelters are located near the hotel or shelter you
will be traveling to. Remember that most shelters will not
allow pets. Four websites to locate places that will accept pets:

          www.petswelcome.com
www.dogfriendly.com
www.travelpets.com
www.petfriendlytravel.com

⚠️ INTERNET 911 FOR PETS

One of the most comprehensive websites I have found for a wide range
of information for helping you resource what you may need to prepare
for pet care before and after disasters is:

          www.pets911.com/index.php

PLANNING PET AND ANIMAL CARE IN EMERGENCIES

IF YOU NEED TO SHELTER YOUR PET

Call your local emergency management office animal shelter or animal control office to get their advice and information. Have copies of veterinarian records and immunizations to leave with the shelter you decide to take your pet to. Have a backup plan because the shelter closest to you may also be affected by the disaster.

FEMA GUIDELINES FOR LARGE ANIMALS

- Ensure all animals have some form of identification.
- Evacuate animals if possible. Plan two possible evacuation routes.
- Make available vehicles and trailers needed for transporting and supporting each animal. Have experienced handlers and drivers. Allow animals to become accustomed to vehicular travel.
- Ensure destinations have food, water, veterinary care, and handling equipment.
- If evacuation is not possible, decide whether to move large animals to shelter or turn them outside.

    If you have experienced a disaster where you live and afterwards find animals that need to be rescued or need shelter, contact Noah's Wish which is a non-profit organization dedicated to rescuing and sheltering animals.

 www.noahswish.org

SAFETY OF FAMILY COMES FIRST

This whole subject is highly emotional for many families. My only admonition is to not place the safety and health of the pet (s) above the well-being and safety of the family members. Evacuating the family with pets may greatly complicate matters. If so, place the pet(s) in a shelter.

BREAD OF LIFE

"I am the bread of life;
whoever comes to me shall not hunger,
and whoever believes in me shall never thirst."

John 6:35

HOPE
FITNESS & NUTRITION

OVERVIEW

IN PART FIVE you will:

+ Be challenged to establish a physical fitness schedule for yourself.

+ Learn about normal body weights for children as well as adults.

+ Learn about BMI (body mass index) and its relationship to your health.

+ Discover free websites to help you get fit.

+ Set personal nutritional goals.

+ Discover free websites to help you get plan your nutritional goals.

+ Be encouraged to have an "accountability partner".

ESTABLISH A PHYSICAL FITNESS PROGRAM

Establish a physical fitness program for yourself and family. Put it in writing for each family member to review and monitor progress! Make this a family accountability item and encourage each other to reach desired goals! Being physically fit may become a matter of avoiding major injury or even death. Check out your risk factors by following the steps listed below.

EVALUATE THE FITNESS OF EACH FAMILY MEMBER
BODY MASS INDEX FOR ADULTS

The National Heart Lung and Blood Institute has a very convenient way for you to evaluate your body mass index (BMI) which is a measure of body fat based on height and weight that applies to both adult men and women. The BMI lists four categories: underweight, normal weight, overweight or obesity. Go to http://www.nhlbi.nih.gov/health/educational/lose_wt/BMI/bmicalc.htm and see what your BMI is! On this site you will find your health risks based on your BMI and also waist circumference.

WAIST CIRCUMFERENCE

Determine your waist circumference by placing a measuring tape snugly around your waist. It is a good indicator of your abdominal fat which is another predictor of your risk for developing risk factors for heart disease and other diseases. This risk increases with a waist measurement of over 40 inches in men and over 35 inches in women.

OTHER RISK FACTORS FOR HEART DISEASE AND OTHER DISEASES

+ high blood pressure (hypertension)
+ high LDL-cholesterol ("bad" cholesterol)
+ low HDL-cholesterol ("good" cholesterol)
+ high triglycerides
+ high blood glucose (sugar)
+ family history of premature heart disease
+ physical inactivity
+ cigarette smoking

ESTABLISH A PHYSICAL FITNESS PROGRAM

IDEAL BODY WEIGHT FOR CHILDREN

There is a website I found that will help answer questions about the ideal body weight for your child(ren) and give practical advice as well:

 http://pediatrics.about.com/cs/growthcharts2/l/bl_ibw_calc.htm.

If you determine that one or more of your children are overweight or not physically fit, discuss a nutritional and physical fitness plan with your pediatrician or family doctor. Children are particularly vulnerable and should not be placed on diets without professional supervision.

TAKE ACTION NOW TO GET FIT

A healthy diet and good fitness program will add years to your life and help you to be ready for emergencies! I recommend you at least visit the website:

 www.exrx.net
if you do not already have an exercise program in place.

Whether you are overweight or elderly or just a "couch potato", the website will help you get started on developing an exercise program that is right for you. Many of the recommendations will not cost you a penny! Try the "Y" (YMCA).

GETTING FIT

1. Determine Body Mass Index of adult family members. www.nhlbi.nih.gov/health/educational/lose_wt/BMI/bmicalc.htm
2. Determine the ideal weight for each child. Consult with the child's doctor for nutritional and fitness advice.
3. Check out www.exrx.net for excellent fitness and nutritional advice.
4. Set realistic goals. Setting and meeting intermediate goals will encourage you. Once initial goals have been met, set new goals.
5. NOW ACT ON WHAT YOU HAVE LEARNED! BE FIT!

NUTRITIONAL GOALS

Put in writing your **nutritional goals**, particularly if you have not been routinely eating a healthy diet. Insert several pages of good dietary plans to be a reminder. You must combine your nutritional goals with your physical fitness goals to make any physical fitness program meaningful.

Consult with your doctor or knowledgeable healthcare professional about recommending a specific dietary plan to follow.

WHOLE FOOD PLANT BASED DIET

In recent years there has been an increasing interest in promoting a whole food plant based diet. A whole-food, plant-based diet is centered on whole, unrefined, or minimally refined plants and consists of fruits, vegetables, tubers, whole grains, and legumes. Those who follow the diet strictly exclude or minimize meat (including chicken and fish), dairy products, and eggs, as well as highly refined foods like bleached flour, refined sugar, and oil. There is an interesting documentary you may watch at: www.forksoverknives.com/the-fok-diet/. It is worth watching even if you do not follow all of the dietary suggestions.

A number of people following the whole food plant based diet have reported benefits in lowering cholesterol, lowering blood pressure, significant weight loss, better diabetic control, better sleeping patterns and an overall better sense of well being.

If you want to develop your own personal dietary plan, consider checking out the following two websites:

www.exrx.net/Nutrition.html
www.health.gov/dietaryguidelines

I do not recommend any fad diets though there are many published diet programs. Good, sensible, consistent eating habits coupled with discipline and exercise is the most successful way to succeed in being physically fit and develop healthy lifestyles. There are commercial programs such as Weight Watchers that have sound nutritional programs, and some people benefit by the interactive nature of the program.

NUTRITIONAL GOALS
NUTRITION PLAN

1. Ask your doctor or nutritionist to recommend a diet for you.

2. If you want to develop your own diet program, check out the following websites:

   www.exrx.net/nutrition.html
   www.exrx.net/nutrition/dietdevelopment.html
   www.health.gov/dietaryguidelines
   www.myhdiet.com/ (whole foods/plant based)

   Let your doctor know what diet plan you have developed.

3. Stick to your diet. Remember several smaller meals daily are better than 1 or 2 large meals.

4. If you are overweight, weigh yourself daily as you follow your nutritional plan.

5. Have someone be your "accountability partner" who will help youkeep "on track".

6. Be sure to exercise as you follow your nutritional plan.

7. Get adequate sleep!

Don't get discouraged. After following the guidelines closely for a few days, you will be able to estimate portions accurately and also become very familiar with the food groups and food exchanges. Once you have learned these nutritional facts well, it will help you and your family the rest of your lives.

9-11, 911, 91:1

THE SECRET CODE FOR BELIEVERS

"He who dwells in the shelter of the Most High
will rest in the shadow of the Almighty.
I will say of the Lord
'he is my refuge and my fortress,
my God, in whom I trust. '
Surely he will save you from the fowler's snare
and from the deadly pestilence.
He will cover you with his feathers,
and under his wings you will find refuge;
his faithfulness will be your shield and Rampart.
You will not fear the terror of night,
nor the arrow that flies by day,
nor the pestilence that stalks in the darkness,
nor the plague that destroys at midday. 1000 may fall at your side,
ten thousand at your right hand,
but it will not come near you.
You will only observe with your eyes
and see the punishment of the wicked."

Psalm 91:1 – 8

HOME SECURITY

OVERVIEW

IN PART SIX you will:

+ Learn tips on securing your home.

+ Receive basic self-defense guidelines.

+ Learn about Neighborhood Watch programs.

+ Identify if you are living in an area with high risk for terrorist acts.

+ Learn basic recommendations on preparing for man-made disasters.

+ Learn about resources for more information on terrorism.

+ Learn that if you are prepared for your disasters common to where you live you will be better prepared for man-made disasters!

+ Be reminded that your best protection is from the LORD!

HOME SECURITY AND PROTECTING YOUR FAMILY

Basically the steps to take for your personal home security, crime prevention and protecting your family are the same before and after a disaster.

A major difference between providing security for your home before and after a disaster is that it may be much more difficult to provide security if there has been much widespread damage. In such situations the National Guard, police and other security personnel often are assigned to patrol affected areas to provide security.

NEIGHBORHOOD WATCH

A good neighborhood watch program would be helpful. Neighbors can look out for each other. Contact some of the neighborhood watch networks in your community to find out how they have planned to handle emergency response and disaster follow up. USAonWatch-Neighborhood Watch has expanded beyond their traditional crime prevention. Check out the National Neighborhood Watch website:

 www.nnw.org/usaonwatch

 Refer to Addendum 2, Who's On First? (Existing Networks), *When All Plans Fail.*

SELF DEFENSE

I approach this subject with reluctance. Everybody has their own their own level of comfort with this topic. I give a few general guidelines and steps on the facing page that I think are prudent. I refer you to Aton Edwards book *Preparedness Now!* for a more in-depth discussion on this topic.

GUARDIAN ANGELS

I have faced very dangerous situations over my years as a medical missionary in 105 nations. I have found my best protection is prayer and being led by the Spirit of the Lord! Psalms says we have guardian angels! Read Psalm 91.

HOME SECURITY AND PROTECTING YOUR FAMILY TIPS

Use Quick Release Locks: Have security locks on all doors, but have locks with quick release mechanisms to quickly exit in case of fire.

Keep Home and Surroundings Well Lit

Home Security Systems: Sophisticated systems tie into the fire and police call centers as well as a home security company. Pricing varies.

Vision at Night: Be very aware people can see in better than you can see out. Expensive items may attract thieves. Close blinds or curtains.

SELF DEFENSE ADVICE

* **Avoid confrontation** if at all possible.
* Take some form of protection such as a **walking stick, cane or sturdy umbrella** should you encounter stray animals (including human)! This is advisable in non-disaster times.
* **Do not walk alone** if chaotic situations exist after a disaster.
* **Pepper spray** with a SHU (Scoville Heat Unit) number of at least 2 million is recommended. Good alternative to firearms.

 www.mace.com or www.zarc.com

* **Use firearms only if you have been extensively trained** by the military or a law enforcement agency.
* Some people say that having a **shotgun for personal defense** at home is the best choice if one is going to have any such weapon.
* **Don't use a toy gun** to scare a would-be attacker.

 Chapter 13, Hang Together or Hang Separately, *When All Plans Fail*

MAN-MADE DISASTERS AND TERRORIST ACTS

 I briefly address these issues in chapter 3, Horses or Zebras (What to Prepare For) in When *All Plans Fail*. Also, pertinent information and websites are given in Appendix A.

As I wrote in the book, terrorism is hard to predict or prepare specifically for various types of terrorists acts, but there are some general recommendations that are given by the DHS/FEMA publication I have referred to earlier, *Are You Ready*. The publication covers explosions, biological threats, chemical threats, nuclear blast, radiological dispersion device (dirty bomb) and the Homeland Security Advisory System. The advice is very easy to read and is a quick resource for terrorism preparedness. Also visit the DHS/FEMA website:

 www.ready.gov and/or download the FEMA app.

The Red Cross website has good information on disaster preparedness including information on terrorism.

 www.redcross.org and/or download the Red Cross Emergency app.

I have chosen not to go into depth on this subject for several reasons. The first is that I want to motivate the 85-90% of the people that are not now prepared. Listing all the various threats and how to prepare for them would more likely produce fear and maybe paralysis and de-motivate people to prepare. Secondly, if you are prepared for your "Horses", that is the common natural disasters, you will be much better prepared should a "Zebra" (man-made disaster) show up.

On these two pages of the workbook I will highlight some of the points I made in the book for quick reference.

PREPARE FOR YOUR HORSES!

YOU WILL THEN BE MUCH BETTER PREPARED FOR ANY ZEBRAS THAT SHOW UP!

GENERAL INFORMATION TO PREPARE FOR

MAN-MADE AND TERRORIST ACTS

Regarding preparing for terrorist acts, you will have to individually determine if you fit into a low, medium or high risk situation for exposure for terrorist acts and take steps to inform yourself about those areas.

Areas of greater risk for Zebras are:
- a large metropolitan area
- government facilities
- international airports
- high-profile land marks

Be prepared to do without services you normally depend on such as electricity, telephone, natural gas, gasoline pumps, cash registers, ATMs and Internet transactions. Plan how you would deal with such problems.

Pay attention more closely to what is going on in the airports Be aware of any unusual behavior. Do not accept packages from strangers or leave luggage unattended.

Consider installing a High Efficiency Particulate Air (HEPA) filter in your return duct of your central heating and cooling system. This would filter out most biological agents that might be used in a terrorist act.

Install water filtration systems for water you drink if you are not already filtering your drinking water.

Be an involved citizen. Notify authorities of any suspicious activity in your neighborhood.

INSTILL FAITH NOT FEAR IN YOUR CHILDREN

Be keenly aware of your children and inform them in an age appropriate way about disaster preparedness.

STASH THE CASH

My cousin's daughter lived in Galveston, Texas. One week before Hurricane Ike came through, she read *When All Plans Fail* and heeded the advice to have cash on hand at home for emergencies. The area where she lived was devastated by the hurricane. She had no access to her bank's automatic teller machine for 10 days!

Following the advice in the book, however, she had made sure to have sufficient funds at home to "weather the storm."

Paul R Williams, M.D.

APPENDICES

APPENDIX A

HAZARD SPECIFIC PREPAREDNESS GUIDELINES

 The information in this workbook Appendix A is taken mainly from Appendix A, Hazard Specific Preparedness Guidelines in *When All Plans Fail*. I have written the information for one common hazard per page to make it easier to remove and place the pages in your personal notebook. This makes it easier to make photocopies as well.

The back of each hazard page either continues with further information on the specific hazard or left blank for you to write notes on that specific hazard.

STATE AND LOCAL INFORMATION FROM FEMA

 www.ready.gov/localized-ready-programs

FEMA WEBSITE FOR HAZARD SPECIFIC INFORMATION

Another excellent FEMA website for hazard specific information is:

 www.ready.gov/natural-disasters

FLOODS

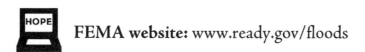 **FEMA website:** www.ready.gov/floods

STEPS TO TAKE TO PREPARE FOR A FLOOD

* If you are at risk for flooding, elevate your furnace, water heater, and electrical panel.

* Consider constructing barriers to stop floodwater from entering your home. Basement walls should be sealed with waterproofing compounds.

* Consider flood insurance.

* Make sure you have a full tank of gas if you anticipate flooding.

*

RESPONDING TO FLOODING

* Know the terms used for flooding hazards. A **flood watch** or **flash flood watch** means there is a possibility of flooding or flash flood in your area. *Be prepared to evacuate.*

* Keep informed by visiting www.weather.gov/briefing/, NOAA Watch or local emergency broadcasts. If the flooding hazard changes to **flood warning** it means a flood is occurring and *you may be advised to evacuate immediately.* A **flash flood warning** means a flash flood is occurring and *you must seek higher ground immediately.*

* Do not walk through moving water if at all possible. Even a small amount of water may knock you down.

* Do not drive into flooded areas. If you get caught by rising water, get out of your vehicle as quickly as you can and move to higher ground.

* Stay away from downed power lines.

* Do not return to your home until authorities say it is safe.

NOTES ON FLOODING

HURRICANES

FEMA website: www.ready.gov/hurricanes

PREPARE FOR HURRICANES

- A **hurricane watch** means a hurricane is possible in your area. Be prepared to evacuate if instructed by authorities.

- A **hurricane warning** is when a hurricane is expected in your area. Evacuate immediately when instructed to do so. If you or family members have special needs, be among the first to evacuate!

- Keep trees near home well trimmed.

- Have car filled with gas

- Secure your property. Bring in all outdoor furniture and items that are not tied down. Cover windows with plywood or hurricane shutters.

- Follow your evacuation plans if told to do so.

- Be sure to let your out of state family know about your plans.

- If you are not able to evacuate for any reason, stay in an interior room that does not have windows if that is possible. Remember there may be a lull in the storm as the eye of the hurricane moves over. Stay in your home until told by authorities it is safe.

- Stay informed by listening to NOAA Weather Radio, watch TV or listen to the radio

NOTES ON HURRICANES

THUNDERSTORMS AND LIGHTNING

 FEMA website: www.ready.gov/thunderstorms-lightning

- Remove dead tree branches or cut down rotting trees that might fall during a severe storm.

- Follow the 30/30 lightning safety rule. If you see lightning and you hear thunder before you count to 30, you should go indoors and remain there for at least 30 minutes after the last clap of thunder.

- If the storm is severe, be sure to follow with the NOAA Weather Radio or other radio station for more weather information.

- Bring in or secure loose outdoor furniture.

- Do not use a corded phone except in an emergency. Cell phones and cordless phones are safe to use.

- Avoid use of computers and TV's during thunderstorms due to the possibility of power surges. Use surge protectors.

- Avoid showering or bathing during a thunderstorm.

- If you are caught outside when a storm hits, seek shelter in a building or automobile.

- If shelter is not available, go to the lowest area close to you, but do not lie on the ground. Avoid hilltops and isolated trees in open fields.

- If you are on open water, get to shore and find shelter immediately.

NOTES ON THUNDERSTORMS AND LIGHTNING

TORNADOES

 **FEMA website:** www.ready.gov/tornadoes

PREPARE FOR TORNADOES

- A **tornado watch** means a tornado is possible in your area. Listen to your NOAA Weather Radio, local radio or TV news.

- A **tornado warning** means a tornado is actually occurring and you need to take shelter immediately.

- Go to the area in your home where you have pre-determined is the safest place.

    - Storm cellar or basement is safest
    - If underground area is not available, go to an interior hallway or interior room on the lowest floor possible. Go to the center of the room and stay away from windows, doors and outside walls.
    - Remain in the sheltered area until the danger has passed.

- If you are caught in your vehicle or in a trailer or mobile home, plan to go to a building with a strong foundation if at all possible.

- If you cannot get to a safe shelter, lie flat in a ditch or low-lying area. Do not get under an overpass or bridge.

- After a tornado do not enter damaged buildings. Watch out for downed power lines and any gas leaks.

- Help injured or trapped people.

- Stay informed regarding the weather conditions and any other emergency broadcast information.

NOTES ON TORNADOES

WINTER STORMS AND EXTREME COLD

 FEMA website: www.ready.gov/winter-weather

+ Make sure your home is well insulated and the weather stripping around doors and windows is in place and in good repair.

+ Have plenty of firewood available if you have a fireplace.

+ Become familiar with the winter weather terms:

> + **Freezing rain** creates a coat of ice on roads, walkways and can destroy trees and vegetation.

> + **Sleet** is rain that turns to pellets of ice. Roads freeze and become very slippery.

> + **Winter Weather Advisory** means that cold, ice and snow are expected.

> + **Winter Storm Watch** indicates that severe weather such as heavy snow or ice is possible within the next 24-48 hours.

> + **Winter Storm Warning** indicates the severe winter conditions have started or will begin soon.

> + **Blizzard Warning** means heavy snow and strong winds will produce a blinding snow, poor visibility, deep snow drifts and life-threatening wind chill.

> + **Frost/Freeze Warning** indicates that temperatures below freezing are expected.

(More information on the back of this page)

WINTER STORMS AND EXTREME COLD (CONTINUED)

If you have been advised to expect a winter storm or extreme cold, then take the following steps:

* Make sure your emergency supplies kit for home, car and personal emergency kit are updated. Be sure adequate clothing and blankets and sleeping bags are part of the preparation.

* Make sure you have adequate food and water supplies for the whole family for a minimum of 3 days, though I recommend at least 2 weeks supply.

* Make sure your vehicle is full of gas.

* Stay informed regarding the weather conditions and any other emergency broadcast information.

NOTES ON WINTER STORMS AND EXTREME COLD

PREPARING FOR EXTREME HEAT

 FEMA website: www.ready.gov/heat

- Make sure your home cooling system is working properly.

- Make sure your home is well insulated and the weather stripping around doors and windows is in place and in good repair.

- Avoid being outdoors during the hottest time of the day.

- Avoid strenuous outdoor activities such as yard work, sports, etc.

- Learn about heat exhaustion and heat stroke.

- Maintain your hydration by drinking plenty of water. Avoid alcoholic beverages.

- Eat light, nutritious meals.

- Wear loose fitting clothing and a hat when outdoors.

- Never leave children or pets alone in closed vehicles.

- Keep informed about weather conditions.

NOTES ON PREPARING FOR EXTREME HEAT

EARTHQUAKES

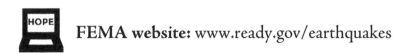 **FEMA website:** www.ready.gov/earthquakes

PREPARING FOR EARTHQUAKES

+ Securely fasten shelves to walls.

+ Store heavier and larger items on lower shelves or in cabinets with latches.

+ Inspect electrical wiring and gas connections and repair if needed.

+ Secure water heater to wall studs with straps and bolt to the floor.

+ Store any flammable or toxic materials in cabinets with doors and latches.

+ Pre-identify safe places in your home or office should an earthquake hit. Getting next to heavy furniture is the best protection from falling debris.

+ Stay away from windows, mirrors and other glass.

+ Avoid exterior walls, exits and areas directly outside of a building where you are at greater risk from falling debris.

+ Be sure you know how to turn off your electricity and gas if needed. Check for gas leaks after an earthquake. If you suspect there is a leak leave immediately and notify the gas company. If possible, turn off the gas outside at the main valve.

+ Expect aftershocks for several hours or even days after the initial earthquake.

NOTES ON EARTHQUAKES

WILDFIRES

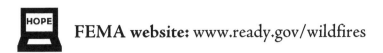 **FEMA website:** www.ready.gov/wildfires

If you live in an area where you know you are at risk for wildfires, go to the FEMA website or American Red Cross for more specific information.

I have included wildfires because it is one of the hazards you need to be ready for emergency evacuation if advised by authorities. Do not return to your home until told by authorities it is safe.

A small sample of the advice you will find on the FEMA website is:

- Create a 30-foot safety zone around the house.

- Create a second zone at least 100 feet around the house.

- Clear all combustibles within 30 feet of any structure.

- Remove debris from under sun decks and porches.

- Enclose eaves and overhangs.

- Install spark arrestors in chimneys and stovepipes.

- Use fire resistant siding.

- Choose safety glass for windows and sliding glass doors.

- Prepare for water storage; develop an external water supply such as a small pond, well or pool.

- Use non-combustible materials for the roof.

- The roof is especially vulnerable in a wildfire. Embers and flaming debris can travel great distances, land on your roof and start a new fire. Avoid flammable roofing materials such as wood and shake shingles. Materials that are more fire resistant include single ply membranes, fiberglass shingles, slate, metal, clay and concrete tile. Be sure to clear gutters of leaves and debris.

NOTES ON WILDFIRES

LANDSLIDES AND DEBRIS FLOW

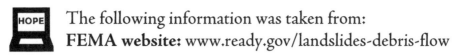

The following information was taken from:
FEMA website: www.ready.gov/landslides-debris-flow

TAKE PROTECTIVE MEASURES BEFORE A LANDSLIDE OR DEBRIS FLOW

The following are steps you can take to protect yourself from the effects of a landslide or debris flow:

- Do not build near steep slopes, close to mountain edges, near drainage ways, or natural erosion valleys.
- Get a ground assessment of your property.
- Consult an appropriate professional expert for advice on corrective measures.
- Minimize home hazards by having flexible pipe fittings installed to avoid gas or water leaks, as flexible fittings are more resistant to breakage (only the gas company or professionals should install gas fittings).

RECOGNIZE LANDSLIDE WARNING SIGNS

- Changes occur in your landscape such as patterns of storm-water drainage on slopes (especially the places where runoff water converges) land movement, small slides, flows, or progressively leaning trees.
- Doors or windows stick or jam for the first time.
- New cracks appear in plaster, tile, brick, or foundations.
- Outside walls, walks, or stairs begin pulling away from the building.
- Slowly developing, widening cracks appear on the ground or on paved areas such as streets or driveways.
- Underground utility lines break.
- Bulging ground appears at the base of a slope.
- Water breaks through the ground surface in new locations.
- Fences, retaining walls, utility poles, or trees tilt or move.
- A faint rumbling sound that increases in volume is noticeable as the landslide nears.
- The ground slopes downward in one direction and may begin shifting in that direction under your feet.
- Unusual sounds, such as trees cracking or boulders knocking together, might indicate moving debris.
- Collapsed pavement, mud, fallen rocks, and other indications of possible debris flow can be seen when driving (embankments along roadsides are particularly susceptible to landslides).

DURING A LANDSLIDE OR DEBRIS FLOW

The following are guidelines for what you should do if a landslide or debris flow occurs:

* Move away from the path of a landslide or debris flow as quickly as possible.
* Curl into a tight ball and protect your head if escape is not possible.

AFTER A LANDSLIDE OR DEBRIS FLOW

The following are guidelines for the period following a landslide:

* Stay away from the slide area. There may be danger of additional slides.
* Check for injured and trapped persons near the slide, without entering the direct slide area. Direct rescuers to their locations.
* Watch for associated dangers such as broken electrical, water, gas, and sewage lines and damaged roadways and railways.
* Replant damaged ground as soon as possible since erosion caused by loss of ground cover can lead to flash flooding and additional landslides in the near future.
* Seek advice from a geotechnical expert for evaluating landslide hazards or designing corrective techniques to reduce landslide risk.

 Follow the instructions for returning home in chapter 13 of *When All Plans Fail.*

NOTES ON LANDSLIDES AND DEBRIS FLOW

VOLCANOES

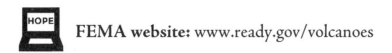 **FEMA website:** www.ready.gov/volcanoes

TAKE PROTECTIVE MEASURES

Before a Volcanic Eruption
- Add a pair of goggles and disposable breathing mask for each member of the family to your disaster supply kit.
- Stay away from active volcano sites.

During a Volcanic Eruption
- Evacuate immediately from the volcano area to avoid flying debris, hot gases, lateral blast, and lava flow.
- Be aware of mudflows. The danger from a mudflow increases near stream channels and with prolonged heavy rains. Mudflows can move faster than you can walk or run. Look upstream before crossing a bridge, and do not cross the bridge if mudflow is approaching.
- Avoid river valleys and low-lying areas.

Protection from Falling Ash
- Wear long-sleeved shirts and long pants.· Use goggles and war eyeglasses instead of contact lenses.
- Use a dust mask or hold a damp cloth over your face to help with breathing.
- Stay away from areas downwind from the volcano to avoid volcanic ash.
- Stay indoors until the ash has settled unless there is a danger of the roof collapsing.
- Close doors, windows, and all ventilation in the house (chimney vents, furnaces, air conditioners, fans, and other vents.
- Clear heavy ash from flat or low-pitched roofs and rain gutters.
- Avoid running car or truck engines. Driving can stir up volcanic ash that can clog engines, damage moving parts, and stall vehicles.
- Avoid driving in heavy ash fall unless absolutely required. If you have to drive, keep speed down to 35 MPH or slower.

NOTES ON VOLCANOES

TSUNAMIS

FEMA website: www.fema.gov/areyouready/tsunamis.shtm

TAKE PROTECTIVE MEASURES

During a Tsunami
The following are guidelines for what you should do if a tsunami is likely in your area:

+ Turn on your radio to learn if there is a tsunami warning if an earthquake occurs and you are in a coastal area.
+ Move inland to higher ground immediately and stay there.

TSUNAMI WARNING SIGN

CAUTION - If there is noticeable recession in water away from the shoreline this is nature's tsunami warning and it should be heeded. You should move away immediately.

After a Tsunami
The following are guidelines for the period following a tsunami:

+ Stay away from flooded and damaged areas until officials say it is safe to return.
+ Stay away from debris in the water; it may pose a safety hazard to boats and people.

NOTES ON TSUNAMIS

HAZARDOUS MATERIALS INCIDENTS

The information on handling biological threats and chemical threats may be found at the following FEMA sites:

 Hazardous Materials Incidents:
www.ready.gov/hazardous-materials-incidents

 Biological Threat:
www.ready.gov/biological-threats

 Chemical Threat:
www.ready.gov/chemical-threats

NOTES ON HAZARDOUS MATERIALS INCIDENTS

BLACKOUTS, SPACE WEATHER: CORONAL MASS EJECTIONS (CMES) AND SOLAR FLARES

Information on blackouts and space weather (coronal mass ejections) can be found at:

 www.ready.gov/blackouts
www.ready.gov/space-weather

 Chapter 11 in *When All Plans Fail*

An extensive list of preparedness supplies for your Grab-and-Go bag and preparations needed in the event of severe space weather is given in Chapter 11 as noted above.

Protecting your sensitive electronic devices and equipment from severe space weather requires some unique preparedness actions.

To protect sensitive electronics take the following steps:

+ Obtain at least two radios that run on 12 V DC power or rechargeable battery packs; create a Faraday cage by storing each radio in its own cardboard box; then put that inside a bigger box and wrap completely with aluminum foil.
+ For your sensitive electronics, build your own Faraday cages or purchase CME-proof bags (place in water proof bags).

There are a number of articles and videos on the Internet that give instructions on how to build your own Faraday cage at home. One such website is:

 www.thesurvivalistblog.net/build-your-own-faraday-cage-heres-how/

NOTES ON BLACKOUTS, SPACE WEATHER: CORONAL MASS EJECTIONS (CMES) AND SOLAR FLARES

NUCLEAR POWER PLANTS, RADIATION
AND NUCLEAR THREATS

Information on nuclear power plant accidents, radiation and nuclear threats may be found at the following FEMA sites:

 www.ready.gov/nuclear-power-plants
www.ready.gov/radiological-dispersion-device-rdd (dirty bomb)
www.ready.gov/nuclear-blast

 Chapter 11 in *When All Plans Fail*

The most important action to take is to become knowledgeable about what to do to protect you and your family. Go to the above websites *and* read chapter 11 of *When All Plans Fail*.

One simple action that you can take readily, is to obtain potassium iodide to help protect the thyroid from radiation injury.

The recommendations of how to prepare for and respond to an EMP are too many and too detailed for this workbook.

In the book I discuss the Lord's Protective Shield. Second Chronicles 7:14 states:

"If my people, who are called by my name, will humble themselves and pray and seek my face and turn from their wicked ways, then will I hear from heaven and will forgive their sin and will heal their land."

NOTES ON NUCLEAR POWER PLANTS, RADIATION AND NUCLEAR THREATS

EBOLA AND THREATS OF PANDEMICS

 See Chapter 10 in *When All Plans Fail.*

Pandemics have occurred historically with the 1918 influenza pandemic being the most catastrophic. More recently there was the scare of a bird flu epidemic in 2005 and, in 2008, the threat of swine flu (H1N1). Neither of these feared epidemics actually materialized.

Most recently the fear of an Ebola epidemic/pandemic riveted public attention. Fortunately, no significant spread of Ebola has occurred in the United States. However, pandemic threats will be faced in the future.

In chapter 10 there is information on the impact of nutrition, exercise and a healthy lifestyle on your ability to combat infections. In addition, there is a list of foods, herbs and other products that have health benefits and may help you fight infections.

MAJOR ALERT! VITAMIN D DEFICIENCY AND INFECTIONS

Vitamin D plays a significant role in achieving a healthy immune system. Studies have shown that individuals with higher vitamin D levels are less likely to contract infections.

In a fairly recent study it was reported that seven out of 10 US children are vitamin D-insufficient! Individuals with darker skin pigmentation, as well as pregnant women, are at greater risk for vitamin D deficiency. Currently 400 IU/day of vitamin D is recommended for children and adolescents. Even more is recommended for pregnant women. Take vitamin D and get at least 20 to 30 minutes of sun daily, if possible!

ELDERBERRY EXTRACT

A recent study reported that Sambucol, a standardized extract of black elderberry has been found to fight avian flu virus (H5N1). Elderberry extracts have been used for years to help treat flu symptoms. According to this study, those taking elderberry supplements recovered in half the time.

When pandemics threaten in the future, you will be faced with making an informed decision for yourself and your family regarding receiving vaccinations. Consult with your healthcare provider.

NOTES ON EBOLA AND THREATS OF PANDEMICS

APPENDIX B

FOOD ITEMS AND STORAGE

 Information is taken from Appendix B in *When All Plans Fail* Reproduced in workbook for easy referencing.

EMERGENCY FOOD SUPPLY CHOICES

For your emergency food supply, choose foods that do not require refrigeration or special preparation. Select foods that require very little water or cooking. Avoid foods that will make you thirsty.

To decide how much food to store, calculate the amount of food you need for two meals per person per day for 2 weeks. The easiest way to do this is to plan a daily menu to help you estimate quantities of food to store. The government only recommends having a 3-day food supply, but that is not realistic for more major disasters.

STORE WHAT YOU EAT, EAT WHAT YOU STORE

As I indicated in earlier in chapter 4, some people recommend 3-6 months of food storage. This gets to be very expensive for many families. Following the "Store what you eat, and eat what you store" principle will allow you to achieve this goal without breaking your monthly budget.

If some of the foods you choose to store are not normally part of your diet, begin to occasionally use these items and learn to prepare them so this preparation becomes routine for you.

ESSENTIAL FOOD STORAGE

FOOD CHOICES

- whole grains: wheat, barley, white or yellow corn, oats, rice (consider buying a grain mill)
- spelt (if you are allergic to wheat and wheat products, spelt can be used in cooking and baking just as you would wheat)
- dried grains
- dried fruit
- beans: black beans, black-eyed peas, chickpeas, kidney beans, lentils, lima beans, navy beans, soybeans, split peas, white beans, pinto beans, peanuts, etc. (beans are very nutritious and can be cooked whole, ground into flour or sprouted)
- nuts, including canned nuts: almonds, black walnuts, brazil nuts, cashews, filberts, pistachios, pecans, peanuts
- seeds: alfalfa, flax, pumpkin, radish, sesame and sun flower – non-salted
- canned foods low in sodium with high liquid content (**do not forget a manual can opener!**)
- powdered milk (boxed)
- dried eggs
- dehydrated foods (learn to dehydrate your vegetables, fruit and meats)
- MREs (Meals Ready to Eat) available in wilderness and sporting good stores
- canning your own fruits and vegetables (canning is a lost art today, but books and classes at preparedness meetings are available)
- freeze-dried foods (the benefit is that some have a shelf life of 25-30 years; the drawback is that water and cooking are required)
- peanut butter
- low-sodium crackers, granola bars, trail mix
- instant coffee, tea
- sweeteners: brown sugar, honey, maple syrup, molasses, sorghum
- salt and other spices
- baking powder, baking soda, yeast, cooking oils

TIPS ON BULK FOOD STORAGE

If you are storing in bulk, 20 pounds of wheat or other grains will feed one person for one month (80 pounds will feed a family of four for one month). Ten pounds of beans will feed one person for one month (40 pounds will feed a family of four for one month). Twenty pounds of powdered milk will feed one person for one month (80 pounds will feed a family of four for one month). Three quarts of oil are needed per month per person.

FOOD STORAGE CONTAINERS

Unless the food you buy is already packaged in a long-term storage package, transfer food into food-grade plastic containers or metal containers with airtight seals to protect from insects and rodents.

Once a bucket or can is opened, be prepared to reseal it. "Gamma Seal" lids work well and allow access to 5- and 6-gallon plastic containers.

Reusable plastic lids are made for number 10 cans. Refer to *Don't Get Caught with Your Pantry Down*, by James Talmage Stevens to source different types of lids.

Store food away from gasoline or other fuels, especially if in plastic containers. Plastic containers may allow odors to penetrate and affect the contents. Also, do not set plastic containers directly on concrete because plastic will absorb moisture.

Remember to:
- Store food in cool, dry area.
- Rotate emergency stocks every 6 to 12 months. (Some items can be stored indefinitely.)
- Include special dietary needs.
- Do consider planting a small garden and/or have garden seeds for vegetables and other foods.
- Do not discuss information about your emergency food and water supply outside of your family.

SAFETY AND SANITATION DO'S AND DON'TS

Do:
- Keep garbage in closed containers and dispose outside, burying garbage, if necessary.
- Discard any food that has come into contact with contaminated flood water.
- Use only pre-prepared canned baby formula for infants or powdered formula with treated water.
- Discard any food that has an unusual odor, color, or texture.

Don't:

- Don't eat foods from cans that are swollen, severely dented, or corroded, even though the product may look safe.
- Don't eat any food that has been at room temperature for two hours. Note: thawed food can usually be eaten if it is still "refrigerator cold." It can be refrozen if it still contains ice crystals. To be safe, remember, "when in doubt, throw it out." This is very conservative advice to minimize any possible food contamination.

ALTERNATIVE COOKING SOURCES

Alternative cooking sources in times of emergency include candle warmers and fondue pots. Charcoal grills and camp stoves are for outdoor use only.

Campfire or fireplace cooking is sometimes referred to as "Dutch oven cooking." If interested in learning more about this technique, go to *www.dutchovencookware.com*.

Solar cooking is also an option. Go to www.solarcookers.org to explore this topic.

CANNED FOODS

Commercially canned food may be eaten out of the can without warming. If you desire to heat the food in the can, be sure the can is thoroughly washed and cleaned first with a disinfectant. Remove any labels from the can and then open the can before heating.

KEEPING FOOD SAFE WITHOUT ELECTRIC POWER

- Look for alternate storage space for your perishable food. (We had to move our frozen foods to a neighbor's home when we lost power for 4 days."
- 20 pounds of dry ice can keep a 10-cubic-foot freezer below freezing for 3-4 days. Handle dry ice carefully with dry gloves to protect your skin.

APPENDIX C

EMERGENCY RESOURCES FOLLOWING DISASTER

 This information is from Appendix L in *When All Plans Fail*

There are many agencies that will provide direct assistance following a disaster. If your church has developed a compassionate ministry program, this would be an excellent place to start.

 Salvation Army:
www.salvationarmy.org

 American Red Cross:
www.redcross.org

FEDERAL ASSISTANCE PROGRAMS

There are many federal assistance programs following disasters. The federal government works in cooperation with state authorities and private firms and together offer a range of disaster insurance, loan and grant programs.

THE FEDERAL EMERGENCY MANAGEMENT AGENCY

 1-800-621-FEMA   www.fema.gov

WHERE TO GO FOR GOVERNMENT DISASTER HELP

One of the first places to go for information related to disaster management, response and recovery is:

 www.fema.gov

FEDERAL CITIZEN INFORMATION CENTER (FCIC)

 Call for questions about federal agencies, programs, benefits and services. 1-800-FED-INFO (1-800-333-4636)

NATIONAL FLOOD INSURANCE PROGRAM

 www.floodsmart.gov/floodsmart/pages/index.jsp.

The NFIP is a cooperative effort between the federal government and private insurance companies.

HOME MORTGAGE INSURANCE

If your home was destroyed or significantly damaged by a presidentially declared natural disaster you may be eligible for home mortgage insurance offered through the Department of Housing and Urban Development (HUD) working through approved lenders.

 http://portal.hud.gov/hudportal/HUD.

The Disaster Voucher Program (DVP) can be accessed at

 http://portal.hud.gov/hudportal/HUD?src=/program_offices/public_indian_housing/publications/dvp

SMALL BUSINESS DISASTER RELIEF LOANS

If you have a small business that was impacted by a presidentially declared natural disaster you may qualify for a disaster relief loan through the Small Business Administration.

Small Business Administration
3rd Street, SW
Washington, DC 20416

 (202) 205-6734

 www.sba.gov

FEDERAL ASSISTANCE TO INDIVIDUALS
AND HOUSEHOLDS PROGRAM (IHP)

You may be eligible for FEMA grants for housing assistance and other serious needs for disaster related expenses such as personal property, transportation, medical, dental or funeral expenses. Go to website:

 www.fema.gov/disaster-survivor-assistance

FEMA TEMPORARY HOUSING PROGRAM

 www.fema.gov/disaster-assistance-available-fema
is the website to go to if you possibly are eligible for this assistance.

1. **Mortgage and Rental Assistance Program**
   If you have received notice of eviction or foreclosure due to financial hardship resulting from a disaster, you may be eligible for assistance.
2. **Rental Assistance**
   If your home has become unlivable due to a disaster, whether you as a homeowner or renter, you may apply for this rental assistance.
3. **Minimal Repairs Program**
   If your home has minor damages but is unlivable as a direct result of a disaster, you may be eligible for money through this program.

DISASTER UNEMPLOYMENT ASSISTANCE

If you lose your job as a result of a disaster and are not eligible for regular unemployment insurance compensation, you may be eligible for this assistance and receive weekly subsidy. If you think you may be eligible for this assistance, go to:

 www.workforcesecurity.doleta.gov/unemploy/disaster.asp

EMERGENCY FOOD COUPONS

You may be eligible for food coupons following a disaster based on your need. The U.S. Department of Agriculture and state authorities administer this program.

APPENDIX D

EMERGENCY PREPAREDNESS FOR NEIGHBORHOODS

 See Chapter 5 and Chapter 14 in *When All Plans Fail*.

CERT

I recommend that you receive preparedness training locally with Community Emergency Response Teams (CERT). Get as many of your neighbors to also have this training.

 www.fema.gov/community-emergency-response-teams

BLS, ACLS AND PALS CERTIFICATION

I also recommend that you obtain basic life support certification (BLS) and even advanced cardio life support certification (ACLS) if you have a healthcare background. Pediatric Advanced Life Support (PALS) is available to healthcare providers that provide emergency care. The certifications can be obtained online.

 www.acls.us

NEIGHBORHOOD WATCH

Consider joining or starting a Neighborhood Watch to better protect your neighborhood and cooperate with local law enforcement officials.

 Learn more at: www.nnw.org
Get their mobile app at www.nnw.org/neighborhood-watch-now!

MAP YOUR NEIGHBORHOOD (MYN)

 Chapter 14 in *When All Plans Fail.*

 mil.wa.gov/emergency-management-
division/preparedness/map-your-neighborhood

- Identify what constitutes your neighborhood.
- Have a neighborhood planning meeting with those neighbors willing to participate (monthly if practical).
- Identify a predetermined meeting place.
- Make special plans to care for the elderly and disabled.
- Special planning will be needed to care for children in the neighborhood.
- Create a skills and equipment inventory of your neighborhood. This will help identify what each neighbor has that would be useful in making any disaster response more effective.
- Create a neighborhood map.
- Create a neighborhood contact list.
- Learn the nine steps to take immediately following a disaster.

I will list only the first six steps to be taken in your own home. Steps 7 through 9 address coming together as a neighborhood.

FIRST SIX STEPS TO BE TAKEN IMMEDIATELY FOLLOWING A DISASTER

1. Take care of your family first. Make sure everyone is OK.
2. Protect your head, hands, and feet. Put on sturdy shoes, leather gloves and a hard hat (or bicycle helmet) to protect from glass and debris.
3. If you are hooked up to gas, inspect the gas meter. If there's any question of smelling gas or you hear it escaping from a broken pipe, immediately shut it off.
4. Shut off your house water at the main house valve. This will trap the water that is in the water heater and keep it safe from pollutants.
5. Post the OK/HELP card on the front door or window.
6. Have your fire extinguisher ready for use either in your home or to help a neighbor.

Learn about the **PREPAREDNESS PEACE MODEL** for neighborhood preparedness in Chapter 14 of *When All Plans Fail.*

RECOMMENDED READING

Publications giving hazard specific preparedness guidelines include:

Williams, Paul R. *When All Plans Fail*, Creation House, Lake Mary, FL, 2015.

Andrews, Harris J. and Bowers, J. Alexander. *The Pocket Disaster Survival Guide*. Accokeek, MD: Stoeger Publishing Company, 2006.

Are You Ready? An in-depth Guide to Citizen Preparedness, published by the Department of Homeland Security/FEMA. Call 1-800-BE-READY or visit the DHS web site www.ready.gov. This publication is free.

Beren, Norris L. *When Disaster Strikes Home!* Mt. Prospect, IL: Emergency Preparedness Educational Institute Publishing, 2004.

Deyo, Holly Drennan. *Dare to Prepare!* Pueblo West, CO: Deyo Enterprises, 2004-2007.

Edwards, Anton. *Preparedness Now!* An Emergency Survival Guide for Civilians and Their Families. Los Angeles, CA: Process Media, 2006.

Kolberg, Judith. *Organize for Disaster*. Decatur, GA: Squall Press, 2004.

Neuenschwander, Mark, M.D., and Neuenschwander, Betsy, M.D. Crisis Evangelism, Preparing to be Salt and Light When the World Needs Us Most. Ventura, CA: Regal Books/A Division of Gospel Light, 1999.

Maloof, F. Michael, *A Nation Forsaken*, WND Books, 2013.

EMERGENCY PREPAREDNESS WEBSITES

www.whenallplansfail.com: emergency preparedness

www.nitro-pak.com: emergency preparedness supplies

www.beprepared.com: emergency preparedness supplies

www.areyouprepared.com: emergency preparedness center

www.emprep.com: emergency preparedness kits and supplies

www.solarsense.com: emergency power systems

www.sundancesolar.com: solar energy products

www.solarcookers.org: solar cooking

www.lovetheoutdoors.com/camping/Outdoor_Cooking.htm: outdoor cooking

www.dutchovencookware.com

www.technonllc.com: emergency escape mask

www.aquamira.com: water purification essentials, and emergency products

www.generalecology.com/category/portable: water filtration, purification

www.nextag.com/money-pouch-travel/products-html: personal pouch

www.firstalert.com/tundra_fire_extinguishing_spray.php: fire extinguisher

www.fireescapesystems.com/products.asp: fire escape systems

www.ingramproducts.com/ezflare or *www.flashpointsafety.com*: flares

www.epipen.com (requires prescription)

mace.com or *www.zarc.com*: personal defense

www.approvedgasmasks.com or *www.airgas.com*: gas masks

www.inflatablerafts.com: inflatable rafts

www.porta-jump.com: car battery charger

www.campmor.com/outdoor/gear/Product____89033?CS_003=2477120&CS_010 =89033: sleeping bags

www.deaf-alerter.com/index.php: deaf alert system

ww.americanmedicalalarms.com: medical alert (blind, deaf, elderly)

www.frio.com.cn/english/comments.asp: keeping medications cool (insulin)

www.exrx.net: exercise/fitness website

www.pets911.com/index.php: website for pet care in emergencies

www.noahswish.org: animal rescue and sheltering

A MESSAGE FROM THE AUTHOR

PAUL R. WILLIAMS, M.D.

TO ALL WHO ARE WISELY PREPARING FOR DISASTERS

As a physician with more than 30 years of medical mission and disaster relief experience, my goal is to equip believers to proactively prepare individually and as a community of believers for natural and man-made disasters. Flooding, hurricanes, tornadoes and earthquakes are increasing in frequency. Also, the threat of terrorism on our soil is ever before us.

Unexpected disasters can add to the personal and societal stresses that we all experience in these changing times. Being prepared spiritually, mentally, and physically allows us to be part of the solution when disasters occur rather than being victimized. We also have a biblical mandate to be prepared.

Please consider hosting a seminar at your church or bringing several churches and community organizations together to sponsor a **When All Plans Fail Seminar**.

The **When All Plans Fail Seminar** is practical teaching on disaster preparedness from a Christian perspective. It is my belief that churches should be places of refuge at all times, especially in times of crisis.

Please let me help you get this important message out. Whether your church decides to host a seminar or not, I encourage you to use my book and workbook as a tool to lead small group studies in your home or in you church to prepare your family, friends and church members. **"The time to prepare is now!"**

Contact me for more information about our mission to prepare and equip believers and churches or to schedule a seminar or speaking engagement.

Looking forward to hearing from you.

Paul R. Williams, M. D.

> **"A prudent man sees danger and takes refuge, but the simple keep going and suffer for it."**
>
> **Proverbs 22:3**

ABOUT THE AUTHOR

Dr. Paul R. Williams received his M.D. from Washington University School of Medicine, St. Louis, Missouri. He was for 15 years on the faculty of the University of South Florida College of Medicine.

Dr. Williams has been involved in full-time medical missions since 1984. He was the founding director of HealthCare Ministries of the Assemblies of God World Missions from 1984 to 1994. Dr. Williams was the first medical director of Operation Blessing in Virginia Beach, Virginia, from 1994 to 1997. In 1997 he founded International HealthCare Network, linking organizations in humanitarian outreaches and ministry. His more than 200 medical mission trips include relief efforts in Bangladesh, Indonesia, Haiti, Philippines, the continent of Africa and other nations. Since 2005 he has been a visiting faculty member of In His Image Family Medicine Residency in Tulsa, Oklahoma.

Dr. Williams and his wife, Sofia, have four children and eight grandchildren.

CONTACT THE AUTHOR

To contact the author to speak at your organization, conference or church, please write to:

Paul R. Williams, MD
International HealthCare Network
PO Box 1180
Pisgah Forest, N 28768

or email:

ihndoc@yahoo.com

For more information visit the author's website: www.whenallplansfail.com.

Examining survivors of the Philippine
typhoon on Island of Mala Pascua

Evaluating the devastation of the
catastrophic tornado in Joplin, MO

Water purification unit provided by Dr.
Williams following Philippine typhoon

St. John's Medical Center devastated by
an EF5 tornado in Joplin, MO

Dr. Williams and Dr. Duininck
coordinating the Indonesian and
American disaster relief teams

Evaluating aftermath of hurricane
Superstorm Sandy in New York

Leading medical relief team in Banda
Aceh, Indonesia following tsunami

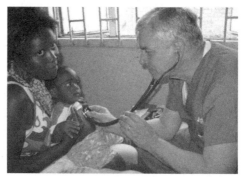

Dr. Williams examines the baby of a
grateful mother in Zambia

THE MISSION

Prepare individuals, neighborhoods and churches to take responsibility for their own preparedness for emergencies and disasters.

Facilitate organizations to respond rapidly to major disasters with humanitarian aid, medical teams, and compassionate ministry.

Mobilize medical teams to bring hope and healing through the love of Jesus to hurting, impoverished people around the world.

Raise Up and Equip the next generation of compassionate ministry leaders.

Integrate the truths of divine healing with practical medicine to meet physical and spiritual needs of others.

Encourage healthcare professionals to use their skills in ministry.

Challenge leaders to greater collaboration for more effective ministry.

International HealthCare Network

TWENTY-ONE DAYS:

TAKE ONE ACTION ITEM EACH DAY

BEGIN NOW! Take ONE action item each day. By the end of twenty-one days, you will have completed the basic requirements for disaster preparedness.

Day 1   Establish a schedule for disaster preparedness.

Day 2   Compile an emergency contact list.

Day 3   Make a list of early warning systems in your community.

Day 4   Identify your "horses," disasters common to your area.

Day 5   Write out your family communication plan in the event of disasters.

Day 6   Make copies of pictures of each family member; store where needed.

Day 7   Make neighborhood preparedness plans.

Day 8   Make lists of items to be included in your emergency kits.

Day 9   Make lists of long-term storage foods; schedule rotation.

Day 10 Make prescription meds list and set up rotation schedule.

Day 11 Make list of emergency supplies not stored in other kits.

Day 12 List first aid kit contents; insert first aid and CPR instructions.

Day 13 Make copies of appropriate important documents.

Day 14 Make copies of immunization records for each family member.

Day 15 Make copies of medical release forms for each child.

Day 16 Make evacuation plans with detailed maps and directions.

Day 17 Write instructions for care of special needs individuals.

Day 18 Make plans for escape routes for fires and post copies in bedrooms.

Day 19 Make plans for caring for animals and pets in emergencies.

Day 20 Establish a physical fitness program.

Day 21 Write out your nutritional goals.

YOU ARE WELL ON YOUR WAY TO BEING PREPARED!